MANGAJIN's
BASIC JAPANESE
through comics

MANGAJIN 's
BASIC
JAPANESE
through comics

A compilation of the first 24 *Basic Japanese*
columns from MANGAJIN magazine

WEATHERHILL
New York • Tokyo

First edition, 1993
First Weatherhill edition, 1998

2 3 4 5 6 7 8 9   09 08 07 06 05 04 03 02 01

Published by Weatherhill, Inc., of New York and Tokyo, with editorial offices at 568 Broadway, Suite 705, New York, New York, 10012, in cooperation with Mangajin, Inc., of Atlanta, Georgia.

Cover art by Ashizawa Kazuko.
Illustrations by Ashizawa Kazuko and Anthony Owsley.
Printed and bound in the U.S.A.

ISBN 0-8348-0452-2

Contents / 目次

Introduction   7

Translating Japanese Manga Into English   8
A discussion of some of the problems facing Japanese-to-English translators, and
some of the methods *Mangajin* uses to handle those problems.

The Manga Market   10
Manga account for over one third of all the books and magazines published in Japan!
This is the rich source of the material presented in *Mangajin*.

Politeness Levels, Pronunciation Guide, and Punctuation Notes   13
A word about the dimensions of "politeness" in Japanese, and notes about our style
of reconciling Japanese and English punctuation.

1 • *Yoroshiku o-negai shimasu* / よろしくお願いします   14
It's one of the most useful expressions in the Japanese language, but you need a little
cultural background.

2 • *Sumimasen* / すみません   20
This versatile expression can be used to express sentiments ranging from "I'm sorry"
to "Thank you."

3 • **Feminine Speech** / 女ことば   26
Some specific examples of the distinctive speech of Japanese women.

4 • *Gaijin* Bloopers / 外人ブルーパー   32
Potential pitfalls for the non-native speaker of Japanese — laugh and learn.

5 • **Hiragana, Katakana and Manga** / ひらがな, カタカナと漫画   34
A brief introduction to written Japanese at the phonetic level.

6 • *Ohayō Gozaimasu & Omedetō Gozaimasu*   42
おはようございますとおめでとうございます — Two idiomatic expressions.

7 • **Creative Kanji Readings** / 当て字（漢字の読み方いろいろ）   48
A device known as *furigana* makes it possible to be creative in assigning readings
to kanji. Manga artists take full advantage of this technique.

8 • *Dōmo*, the All-Purpose Word / 便利なことば「どうも」   54
A polite, easy-to-pronounce word that can be used in almost any situation.

9 • *Dōzo* / どうぞ   60
It means "please," but only in certain situations.

10 • *Baka*, the Basic Insult / 「ばか」の使い方   66
Even if you never plan to insult anyone, it's good to know something about the
concept of *baka*.

11 • *Shitsurei* / 失礼   72
It means "rudeness" or "impoliteness," and it's used especially by people with impeccable manners.

12 • *Ii,* **the "Good" Word /** 「いい」のいろいろ   **78**
A handy word, but it can sometimes cause confusion, even among native speakers.

13 • *Yatta!* **the Exclamation /** 「やった！」   **84**
This spontaneous expression of joy can make your Japanese sound better than it really is.

14 • Saying Goodbye / わかれの言葉   **90**
Sayōnara is only the beginning. There are a number of ways to say goodbye in Japanese; we show you the easiest and most widely used.

15 • The Concept of *Komaru* / 「困る」ということ   **96**
If you're troubled, distressed, or caught in a tight spot, we have a word for you.

16 • Counters and Classifiers / 助数詞   **102**
The straight scoop on counting in Japanese.

17 • Baby Talk / 幼児語   **108**
An introduction to Japanese Toddler-ese; words used only by small children, how babies tend to mispronounce some sounds, and how adults tend to talk to babies.

18 • Informal Politeness / もうひとつのていねい語   **114**
The word "politeness" is a convenient simplification; there are actually several dimensions involved.

19 • Introductions / 紹介   **118**
In practice, introductions use an almost random mix of a few basic elements. We take a look at the elements, and show a few variations.

20 • *"–sama"* **words /** 「様」のさまざま   **124**
Essentially untranslatable, these expressions are part of the unique flavor of the Japanese language.

21 • Hesitating with *anō* / 「あのォ...」   **130**
A little like "Uhh . . ." in English, but possibly more polite, you can get a lot of mileage out of *anō.*

22 • The Wide World of *Desu* / 「です」の世界   **136**
It means "is," but it's much more than that. *Mangajin* looks at some Japanese expressions that non-native speakers probably wouldn't come up with on their own.

23 • *Hai* **(Part I) /** はい（その１）   **142**
"Yes, this isn't a pen" sounds perfectly logical in Japanese.

24 • *Hai* **(Part 2) /** はい（その２）   **148**
In addition to "Yes" (and sometimes "No"), *Hai* can be used as "I hear you," or as an indication that you intend to answer a question.

Vocabulary Index   **156**

Introduction

This book is a collection of material from the Basic Japanese column of *Mangajin* magazine, issues No. 1–24. It is intended as an entertaining supplement to a more formal or structured study of Japanese. *Basic Japanese* does not presume to serve as an introduction to the Japanese language. The 24 "lessons" in this book do not build on each other — each stands independently, and they can be read or studied in any order.

The name *Mangajin* is a play on two Japanese words, *manga* (漫画,"comics") and *jin* (人"people"). It sounds like the English word "magazine" as rendered in Japanese — *magajin* (マガジン). *Mangajin* magazine uses authentic manga, the famous comics which are so immensely popular in Japan, to present the Japanese language as it is really spoken, and to give its readers an inside view of contemporary Japanese society.

Manga may mean "comics," but in Japan they are serious business. Unlike American-style comics, manga are not just "kid stuff" but a highly developed medium for entertainment and education, popular among adults as well as children. It is estimated that manga account for over 1/3 of all books and magazines published in Japan. Because they are so widely read, manga are as powerful as TV in shaping popular culture, and play an integral role in forming national attitudes, starting national fads, and shaping the national language in Japan. A growing number of government agencies, and some of the biggest names in corporate Japan, are now even using manga in training materials, product manuals and corporate histories.

Each issue of *Mangajin* features excerpts from Japan's most popular manga. Facing the manga are complete English translations with notes on vocabulary and grammar, as well as explanations of cultural nuance.

Most of the manga material in *Mangajin* is presented as a story — a complete chapter, or a complete 4-frame manga — but the Basic Japanese column takes a slightly different approach. A particular word, phrase or concept is selected as a theme, and our "manga markers" go through small mountains of manga periodicals searching for examples of that usage. The marked examples are reviewed by the editorial staff and examples are selected that 1) communicate visually the context and situation, 2) are visually interesting, 3) are not atypical usage. The examples are then organized into a flow or pattern, and the translation and annotation is done.

The Basic Japanese column has always been one of the most popular features of *Mangajin* magazine. Since the examples are "real" Japanese, some of the material is fairly advanced (and thus valuable even to advanced students), but it is always made accessible even to basic beginners. In almost all cases, a complete, "4-line" format is used for the translation.

これ	は	一例	です。	original Japanese
Kore	*wa*	*ichi-rei*	*desu.*	reading/pronunciation
this	(subj.)	one-example	is	word-for-word/literal translation
This is an example. (PL3)				final translation (politeness level)

One of the more socially significant differences between English and Japanese is the existence of what can be called "politeness levels" in Japanese. Since these generally have no counterpart in English, we use codes, such as the (PL3 — "Politeness Level 3") at the end of the example above, to indicate the level of politeness. This system is explained in detail on page 13.

We also provide a pronunciation guide on page 13, but if you ever intend to actually speak any of material presented here, you'll probably require some additional help, preferably from a qualified teacher. *Mangajin* magazine is found in select bookstores or can be ordered by calling 1-800-552-3206.

Acknowledgments:

This book includes material from Shogakukan, Kodansha, Take Shobo, Scholar, Futabasha, Shueisha, and other publishers. The publishing business in Japan is very competitive, and these companies have a strong sense of rivalry. We thank them for cooperating in this project and allowing us to combine their material in one volume. In conjunction with the matter of copyrights and permissions, we thank Moteki Hiromichi, the head of Sekai Shuppan Kenkyu Center, *Mangajin*'s representative in Japan for his efforts in securing permission from these publishers.

The people who originally created this material for *Mangajin* magazine include Vaughan Simmons, Wayne Lammers, Karen Sandness, Ben Beishline, Virginia Murray, and the entire *Mangajin* staff.

TRANSLATING JAPANESE *MANGA* INTO ENGLISH

by Vaughan P. Simmons,
Editor & Publisher, *Mangajin* magazine

When I first started developing the prototypes that led to *Mangajin* magazine, I was told by more than one person that although manga might seem rather simple, the language was actually very difficult and it was not realistic to try to use manga as a learning medium for students of Japanese. My reaction was that the language only seemed difficult because no one had really tried to explain it in a systematic fashion before.

The key word here is "explain." In *Mangajin*, we have the luxury of being able to include notes about the language and even intermediate translations, if necessary. The 4-line (and occasionally 5-line) format, which we use whenever space permits, allows us to show both a literal translation and a final translation. It is especially helpful in showing the difference in word order, or what could be called the "linguistic logic." Trying to translate manga without supplying any notes or explanations can be more challenging and even more time-consuming than presenting the complete notes that we provide in *Mangajin*.

One thing that makes life easier for us is that we are very clear about the purpose of our translations, which is to reflect what is really going on in the original Japanese rather than to give the smoothest possible English translation. We have received criticism for this approach from people, mostly manga fans in the US, who dislike seeing their favorite manga characters speaking in "unnatural" English. Our response is that the characters are Japanese and they sometimes express thoughts or concepts which do not exist in English. If these thoughts or concepts are glossed over to sound smooth in English, then the characters have lost their true Japanese persona — they have essentially become American. A good example of this is the expression *Yoroshiku o-negai shimasu*, which, although it has English counterparts in some situations, usually expresses sentiments which are purely Japanese.

One of our special concerns in translating manga is that there is no good way to indicate the different levels of politeness or formality that exist in Japanese. This could conceivably cause embarrassment to a beginning learner who "picked up" a casual expression from a manga story and used it in the wrong situation. In some cases, it is possible to reflect the politeness (or rudeness) of a given expression by altering the wording in English. In most cases, however, we must resort to a series of "PL" (Politeness Level) tags at the end of the sentence. Even this approach, clumsy as it may seem, is not complete. The word "politeness" is an oversimplification of several dimensions (formality of the situation, respect for the person spoken about, relation of the speaker to the other parties, etc.) that are involved in Japanese *keigo* (敬語) or other speech distinctions.

Perhaps the best way to discuss the problems in translating manga is to look at a specific example. The example we have selected is from the series *Obatarian*. (Facing page →)

In the first frame, the word *Obatarian* illustrates one problem Japanese-English translators must learn to handle. The distinction between singular and plural, which must be clear in English, is generally not made in Japanese. In this series, there are several characters who are referred to as *Obatarian*, i.e., it is used as a generic term. In addition, each of the characters is referred to individually as *Obatarian*. This lack of distinction between singular and plural presents no particular problems in Japanese; it is only when translating into English that one must (sometimes arbitrarily) assign a number to the noun. For this first line of narration, we had to decide if the manga artist was referring to this particular *Obatarian*, or to *Obatarians* in general. We felt that the latter was more likely, but really, only the artist could say for sure.

In this area of singular vs. plural, English is more precise than Japanese, but also in this first frame is an example of the opposite case. The expression *kite-iku* (着ていく) makes it clear that they will be going out somewhere (although one could argue that this is clear from the context). In the English, however, there is no natural way to include the concept of "go" which is expressed by *iku*. Fortunately, in *Mangajin*, we can include this in our third line of word-for-word translations.

The distinction between masculine and feminine speech in Japanese is another characteristic that is difficult to reflect in English translation. As is the case with "politeness," this can sometimes be approximated by changing the wording in English, but there is really no satisfactory way to "translate" feminine speech such as the sentence ending *wa* (わ) in the third frame of this manga. Again, we are able to add the note (fem.) in the third line of our format, but this is a luxury unavailable to most translators.

A similar situation exists for the various words used for "I/me" in Japanese. In the last frame, the husband refers to himself as *washi* (わし), but there is no way in English to reflect the myriad terms that are used in Japanese to refer to oneself (*watakushi, watashi, atashi, boku, ore,* etc.) much less the various words for "you" (*anata, otaku, kimi, omae,* etc.).

Differences in colloquialisms, such as *Urusai!* corresponding to "Be quiet!" (in this case), or . . . *nani ga warui?* becoming "What's wrong . . .?" could be problems for the inexperienced translator, but are not especially noteworthy here.

In closing, let me mention one technique that we use when attempting to translate tricky passages. First, say the Japanese out loud (or at least move your mouth and try to adopt a suitable facial expression); then, try saying various English expressions and see what flows naturally. It is surprising how often a fairly literal translation passes this "test," but when it doesn't, it's necessary to come up with a "cultural equivalent" rather than a translation.

Looking at the current readership of *Mangajin* magazine, which includes a high percentage of beginning students as well as teachers, translators, and "language professionals," I would venture to say that we have managed to make "manga-speak" accessible to a wider range of readers than was previously thought possible.

オバタリアン
OBATARIAN
by
堀田かつひこ
Hotta Katsuhiko

The name *Obatarian* was coined from the two words *obasan* (literally "aunt" but also used as a generic term for middle-aged/adult women), and *Batarian* (the Japanese title for the American movie *Return of the Living Dead* — a reference to the "battalions" of zombies in the film). It refers to the type of middle-aged terror shown in this manga, and has now become a part of the Japanese language.

1

Narration: オバタリアン は コーディネイトできない
Obatarian　　　wa　kōdineito　　　　dekinai
obatarians　　as-for　coordinate　　　cannot
Obatarians can't coordinate (their outfits). (PL2)

Arrows: 紫　　　緑
Murasaki　Midori
Purple　Green

Husband: そ それ 着て いくの か?
So sore　kite　iku　no　ka
th- that　wear-and go　(explan.) ?
"You're going to wear that?" (PL2)

- *dekinai* is the plain/abrupt negative form of *dekiru* ("can/able to do").
- *kite* is the *-te* form of *kiru* ("put on/wear" for clothing that involves putting arms through sleeves). *Kite iku* is literally "put on and go" → "wear."
- asking a question with *no ka* shows he is seeking an explanation.

2

Arrow: 茶
Cha
Brown

Husband: そ その くつ はく の か?
So sono kutsu haku no　ka
th- those　shoes　wear　(explan.) ?
"You're going to wear those shoes?" (PL2)

- *haku* means "put on/wear" for apparel one puts one's legs or feet into/through, including pants, stockings, and shoes.

3

Obatarian: うるさい わ ねー
Urusai　　　wa　ne—
noisy/bothersome (fem.) (colloq.)
"Oh, be quiet!" (PL2)

気に入ったもの 着て 何 が 悪い のよーっ
Ki ni itta　　mono kite　nani ga　warui no　yo—!
like(d)　　things wear　what (subj.) is bad (expl) (emph)
"What's wrong with wearing things I like?" (PL2)

えらそう に!! 自分 は どうなの!! えーっ!!
Erasō　　ni!! Jibun wa　dō na no　E—!
air of importance with　yourself as-for how (explan. ?) Hunh?
"You talk like an authority, but how about yourself? Hunh?" (PL2)

- *urusai!* when spoken sharply is equivalent to English "Shut up!/Be quiet!" *wa* is a colloquial particle used mostly by women, and *ne* in this case serves as emphasis: "You sure are noisy" → "Shut up!/Be quiet!"
- *ki ni itta* is the past form of *ki ni iru*, an expression meaning "to like/be pleased with." *Ki ni itta mono* = "things I am/you are pleased with"
- *erasō* is the adjective *erai* ("eminent/important [person]") with the suffix *-sō* indicating "an air/appearance of," so *erasō ni* implies "[act/speak] with an air/appearance of importance/authority."

4

Husband: わし は 大丈夫
Washi wa　daijōbu
I/me　as-for safe/all right
"I'm safe..." (PL2)

Husband: これ 一着 しか ない から...
Kore　itchaku　shika　nai　kara
this　one suit/outfit other than don't have because
"... (because) I only have this one suit." (PL2)

- *washi* is a word for "I/me" used mostly by middle-aged and older men.
- *itchaku* combines *ichi* ("one") and *-chaku*, the counter suffix for suits.
- *shika* followed by a negative later in the sentence means "only."
- *nai* is the negative form of *aru* ("have/exist"), so *(itchaku) shika nai* means "have only (one suit)."

The MANGA MARKET

This is an updated, abridged version of an article which orignally appeared in *Mangajin* magazine No. 9, April 1991.

There are plenty of theories about why manga ("comics") are so popular in Japan. Without getting into theories, here are some facts about the manga market, and the fact is, it's big.

How big is the manga market in Japan? Fortunately, the 出版科学研究所 *Shuppan Kagaku Kenkyūjo* (Publishing Science Research Institute) in Tokyo has plenty of statistics. Total sales of comic or manga-type publications (books as well as magazines) in 1992 were approximately ¥540,000,000,000.

That's five hundred forty billion yen, or more than five billion dollars, and it represents 23 percent of all magazine and book sales in Japan. Manga tend to be on the lower end of the price spectrum, however, and if you look at the number of copies shipped, manga books and magazines accounted for 38 percent of the total (see chart on right).

Circulation figures for manga magazines can be astronomical. For example, the most popular of all manga magazines, 少年ジャンプ *Shōnen Janpu (Jump)*, has a weekly circulation of 5-6 million (mostly males age 12 – early 20s). By comparison, in the US, which has twice the population of Japan, *Time* magazine has a circulation of 4.3 million, and *People* magazine 3.4 million. *Jump* is an exceptional case, but all of the top ten best selling manga magazines in Japan have circulations of over one million.

Volume is high, but profit margins are low. Most manga magazines have 300-400 pages and sell for around ¥220. Advertising content is low by general magazine standards, and all retail outlets can return unsold copies (typically 15-20 percent). The real money in the manga business is made from 単行本 *tankōbon,* or collections of serialized manga in book form.

Because of the low price and high page count, manga magazines are printed on very cheap paper which starts to yellow and deteriorate in a matter of months. This makes the tankōbon, which are printed on better quality paper, a necessity for any collector or loyal reader who wants to re-read past episodes. Tankōbon are typically 150-220 pages and contain 10-15 episodes or installments of a series. Prices are usually about ¥500, but since the contents are "recycled" from magazines, profit margins are high.

One episode in a manga series is around 20 pages, and a typical 340+ page magazine contains 15 or so episodes. Thus, a weekly manga magazine produces enough material for 5-6 tankōbon every month. In this sense, manga magazines are like "farms" to produce material for the more profitable tankōbon sales.

Since manga artists must usually hire several assistants in order to meet the tight production schedules of manga magazines, it's hard for them to make much money from the magazine side of the business, and they rely on sales of tankōbon for their profits as well.

Tankōbon also produce some amazing numbers. The 8th volume in the popular *Be-Bop High School* series had a first printing of 2,360,000 copies, and there have been several other instances of

The publishing pie

38% of all books and magazines published in Japan in 1989 were manga.*

Weekly magazines

Manga

Books

16%

12%

38%

34%

28%	Books
30%	Monthlies
42%	Weeklies

Monthly Magazines

*by number of copies; total book and magazine shipments in 1989, 6.08 billion copies. Source: Shuppan Kagaku Kenkyūjo

The marketplace

Higher postal rates and the fact that most manga magazines are printed on cheap, bulky newsprint-type paper make magazine subscriptions almost non-existent. Practically all magazine and sales are through retail outlets. Retail shops receive goods on consignment from wholesalers and can return any unsold goods.

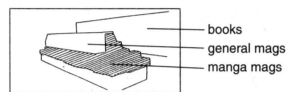

This is the bookstore section of a Daiei "GMS" (General Merchandise Store—a combination of department store and supermarket) in Himonya, Tokyo. Himonya is a rather upscale residential area and this display is more spacious than the typical bookstore, but customers include a demographic cross section.

books
general mags
manga mags

This is a kiosk or 駅売店 *eki-baiten.* There are approximately 4,500 of these in railway stations (often on the platforms) in Japan. These offer a convenient way for salarymen on the go to pick up some light reading material for their train ride.

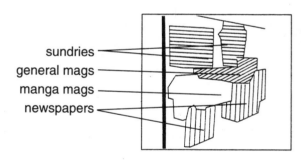

sundries
general mags
manga mags
newspapers

Ratio of manga magazine sales to total magazine sales (by volume/number of copies sold in 1992)

Weekly Magazines

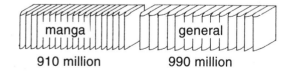

manga
910 million

general
990 million

Monthly Magazines

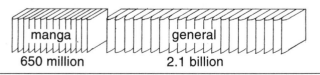

manga
650 million

general
2.1 billion

first printings of over two million copies. Compare this with the 100,000 copy threshold for "best seller" status in the non-manga book business, and the appeal of the manga business becomes obvious.

In these profitable tankōbon sales, the top five publishers in Japan—Shūeisha, Shōgakukan, Kōdansha, Hakusensha, and Futabasha—together have an estimated 78 percent of the market. Their size, stability and history of success make it easy for these big five to monopolize the top manga artists, and thus maintain their position. It's very difficult for new publishers to break into the market.

The *maku-no-uchi bentō* approach: The *maku-no-uchi bentō* (幕の内弁当) is a popular kind of "box lunch" containing a variety of items such as fish, chicken, vegetables, pickles, etc., along with the staple, rice. Publish-

The product comes in 2 sizes:
Big   Bigger

Big Comic (Shōgakukan), ¥230

Estimated circulation: 1.2 million
Primary readership: Adult males, average age over 30, extending into 40s. (Shōgakukan's manga magazines are segmented more by age than Shūeisha's).

The Sep 25,1993 issue (298 pages) includes:

13 stories on subjects such as a hired assassin, a car manufacturer employee, samurai drama, the hotel business, "gag"/slapstick manga, Old World European war. Also some editorial content.

Promo blurbs for coming features, contests, other Shōgakukan publications, etc.   26 pages

Ads for: Energy drinks, jewelry, English lessons, cigarettes, cars, fitness equipment, whiskey, banks, medical clinics   14 pages

Shōnen Jump (Shūeisha), ¥200

Estimated circulation: 6 million
Primary readership: Males, mostly age 12 through early 20s, but extending into 30s and down to 8 or so.

The Aug 9, 1993 issue (446 pages) includes:

19 stories including Last Action Hero, Dragon Ball, and stories on subjects such as basketball, baseball, delinquent high school students, psychic/occult, martial arts, talking monkeys, motorcycle gangs, SF/fantasy.

Promo blurbs for coming features, giveaways, other Shūeisha publications, etc.   45 pages

Ads for: Skin care products, movies and licensed items, watches, board games, hair removal, video games, guitars, bodybuilding/fitness equipment, soft drinks   16 pages

ers of *seinen* 青年 manga (for young males) frequently compare their product to a maku-no-uchi bentō—there is a wide variety of items to appeal to every taste, and even though some people might dislike carrots, they are included to give a touch of color. The most important part, however, is the rice—the part that appeals to everyone. The conventional wisdom is that each manga magazine must contain at least three stories that fit in the "rice" category. If there is only one "rice" story, people will read it standing up (called *tachi-yomi* 立ち読み) at the bookstore/magazine stand without purchasing the magazine. Takahashi Rumiko's *Ranma 1/2* and the popular "gourmet manga" *Oishinbo* are typical "rice" manga.

Many manga magazines have survey cards for the readers to evaluate the stories in that issue. A new series typically has ten weeks to show a good response, or it's history.

Just to survive in this intensely competitve market, manga artists and publishers have to stay in close touch with the popular pulse. For this reason, manga open a window on Japanese popular culture and provide a unique medium for learning about Japan. *Mangajin* magazine and consequently *Basic Japanese Through Comics* draw primarily from this source—large circulation, mainstream manga magazines—to ensure that the language is natural and that authentic cultural context is supplied.

Politeness Levels

The **politeness levels** found in Japanese frequently have no counterpart in English. This can cause problems for translators. The words *suru* and *shimasu* would both be rendered simply as "do" in English, but in Japanese there is a very clear distinction between the "politeness" levels of these two words. In a more extreme case, *shiyagaru* would also be translated simply as "do" in English, but in Japanese this word is openly offensive. To avoid confusion or embarrassment, we label our translations using the codes on the left.

Learning Japanese from manga is a good way to get a feel for these politeness levels. You see words used in the context of a social setting.

The danger in "picking up" Japanese is that even though most Japanese people appreciate the fact that you are interested in learning their language and will give you "slack" as a beginner, misused politeness levels can be pretty grating on the Japanese ear, even if they do not reach the point of being truly offensive.

How can I be safe? Politeness Level 3 can be used in almost any situation. Although it might not be completely natural in a very formal situation, it will not cause offense. If you want to be safe, use PL2 only with friends and avoid PL1 altogether.

These levels are only approximations: To simplify matters, we use the word "politeness," although there are actually several dimensions involved (formality, deference, humility, refinement, etc.). While the level of respect (or lack of it) for the person spoken to or spoken about can determine which words are used, verb forms are determined largely by the formality of the situation. Thus, it is difficult to label the verb *irassharu* (informal form of an honorific verb) using this simple four-level system. In such cases we sometimes use combined tags, such as (PL4-3).

Rather than trying to develop an elaborate system which might be so confusing as to actually defeat the purpose, we feel that this system, even with its compromises, is the best way to save our readers from embarrassing situations.

Codes used in *Mangajin*

(PL4) Politeness Level 4: Very Polite
Typically uses special honorific or humble words, such as *nasaimasu* or *itashimasu*.

(PL3) Politeness Level 3: Ordinary Polite
Typified by the verb *desu*, or the *-masu* ending on other verbs.

(PL2) Politeness Level 2: Plain/Abrupt
For informal conversation with peers.
- "dictionary form" of verbs
- adjectives without *desu*

(PL1) Politeness Level 1: Rude/Condescending
Typified by special words or verb endings, usually not "obscene" in the Western sense of the word, but equally insulting.

Pronunciation Guide

Pronunciation is probably one of the easier aspects of Japanese. Vowel sounds don't vary as they do in English. While English uses the five letters a,e,i,o,u to make 20 or so vowel sounds, in Japanese there are 5 vowels and 5 vowel sounds—the pronunciation is always constant. There are only a few sounds in the entire phonetic system which will be completely new to the speaker of English.

The five vowels in Japanese are written a,i,u,e,o in *rōmaji* (English letters). This is also the order in which they appear in the Japanese kana "alphabet." They are pronounced:

a	like the *a* in f*a*ther, or h*a* ha!
i	like the *i* in macaron*i*
u	like the *u* in z*u*lu
e	like the *e* in g*e*t, or *e*xtra
o	like the *o* in s*o*lo

The length of time that a vowel sound is held or sustained makes it "long" or "short" in Japanese. Don't confuse this with what are called long or short vowels in English. The long vowel in Japanese has exactly the same pronunciation as the short vowel, but it's held for twice as long. Long vowels are designated by a dash over the vowel (*dōmo, okāsan*), or by repeating the vowel (*iimasu*).

The vowels *i* and *u* are sometimes not fully sounded (as in the verb *desu* or the verb ending *-mashita*). This varies between individual speakers and there are no fixed rules.

Japanese consonant sounds are pretty close to those of English. The notable exception is the *r* sound, which is like a combination of the English *r* and *l*, winding up close to the *d* sound. If you say the name Eddie and touch the tip of your tongue lightly behind the upper front teeth, you have an approximation of the Japanese word *eri* ("collar").

Doubled consonants are pronounced by pausing just slightly after the sound is formed, and then almost spitting out the rest of the word. Although this phenomenon does not really occur in English, it is somewhat similar to the *k* sound in the word bookkeeper.

The *n* sound: When it is not attached to a vowel (as in *na,ni,nu,ne,no*), *n* is like a syllable in itself, and as such it receives a full "beat." When *n* is followed by a vowel to which it is not attached, we mark it with an apostrophe. Note the difference between the word for "no smoking," *kin'en* (actually four syllables: *ki-n-e-n*) and the word for "anniversary," *kinen* (three syllables: *ki-ne-n*).

The distinctive sound of spoken Japanese is partly due to the even stress or accent given to each syllable. This is one reason why pronunciation of Japanese is relatively easy. Although changes of pitch do occur in Japanese, in most cases there are not essential to the meaning. Beginners are probably better off to try for flat, even intonation. Rising pitch for questions and stressing words for emphasis are much the same in English.

Punctuation Notes

Most manga artists are very creative with punctuation, and many omit punctuation at the ends of lines, or choose to use no punctuation at all. We sometimes alter the punctuation used by the artist or add punctuation as an aid to comprehension.

In our 4-line format in which the Japanese text (kanji and kana) is reproduced in the notes, we may add standard English punctuation to the first (Japanese) line, if it clarifies the structure of the sentence. For example, if a complete thought is followed by . . ., we usually replace the . . . with a period.

In the second line of our 4-line format (*rōmaji*), we generally follow standard English punctuation. In written Japanese, a small *tsu* (っ) is sometimes placed at the end of a word to show that it is cut off sharply. We usually indicate this with an exclamation mark in English.

In the third line (word-for-word literal translation), we generally use no punctuation, except periods for internal abbreviations and (?) to indicate the function of the "question marker" か (*ka*).

The punctuation used in our final translations is actually an integral part of the translation. We may add an exclamation mark, question mark, or other punctuation to express the content and feel of the original Japanese.

Lesson 1 • *Yoroshiku o-negai shimasu*

Yoroshiku o-negai shimasu is one of the most useful expressions in the Japanese language, but a complete understanding requires some knowledge of Japanese culture because in many situations there is no equivalent English expression.

It drives translators crazy! Students of Japanese usually first encounter *Yoroshiku o-negai shimasu* (or one of its variations) in the dialogue of a personal introduction, where it is typically "translated" as "Pleased to meet you." This is really more of a "cultural equivalent" than a translation, since *Yoroshiku o-negai shimasu* makes no specific mention of "meeting," and its use is certainly not limited to introductions. In an introduction, the translator at least has this option. In some of the situations illustrated on the following pages, it's difficult to come up with a translation or a "cultural equivalent." Word-by-word, it looks something like this:

よろしく

yoroshiku is the adverb form of the adjective *yoroshii*, a rather formal and polite word for "good/nice," so *yoroshiku* literally means "well/favorably." Adjectives which end in *-i* can be made into adverbs by changing *-i* to *-ku.*

> 早い (*hayai*) = quick, rapid   → 早い汽車 (*hayai kisha*) = a fast train
> 早く (*hayaku*) = quickly, rapidly → 早く食べる (*hayaku taberu*) = eat quickly

You might hear *yoroshii* used by an employee asking the boss's approval — *Yoroshii desu ka?* "Is it all right?" in the sense of "May I . . . ," as well as "Is this satisfactory/good (enough)?"

(お)願い

(o)-negai is the noun form of the verb *negau/negaimasu* = "make a request," so it means "(a) request." The *o-* on the beginning is an honorific prefix, somewhat like the *o-* in *ocha.* The *-masu* form of a verb, minus *-masu,* is sometimes called the stem of the verb, and is used like a noun.

> 心からの願い (*kokoro kara no negai*) = literally "a request/wish from the heart."

します

shimasu is the ordinary polite form of the verb *suru,* an all-purpose verb frequently used with nouns to mean "do/make."

> 電話 (*denwa*) = telephone   →   電話します (*denwa shimasu*) = "(I will) call on the telephone."
> じゃま (*jama*) = nuisance/bother →   おじゃまします (*o-jama shimasu*) = literally "(I will) bother (you)," said when entering someone's home or office.

お願いします

o-negai shimasu is a fairly polite way of making a request. It can be used for ordering in a restaurant — *Biiru o-negai shimasu* ("Beer please."), when dropping off laundry — *Kore o o-negai shimasu* ("Please [take care of] these."). It's also used after you have made a request or left a matter in someone's hands.

Perhaps you can see from the above that the three words *Yoroshiku o-negai shimasu* mean something like "Please give me your favorable consideration." It's probably more useful, though, to look at some of the situations where this expression is used.

Introductions

In this story, a woman makes a trip to China to search for the two sons she had left there when war broke out. The guide/interpreter (who is actually one of the sons) has come to her hotel room, and she introduces herself.

The verb *shimasu* is used in "ordinary polite speech" (what is called PL3 in MANGAJIN), and will suffice for most situations.

© Yajima & Hirokane / *Ningen Kōsaten*, Shogakukan

<u>Matsukawa</u>: 松川　　とよ　です。
Matsukawa Toyo desu.
"I'm Matsukawa Toyo."

よろしく　お願い　します。
yoroshiku o-negai shimasu.
"Pleased to meet you." (PL3)

- this woman is employing the guide/interpreter, so as the "boss" she could use the informal *Yoroshiku,* but as middle-aged women typically do, she has added *o-negai shimasu.*
- in addition to the social implications of the introduction, she is also saying *Yoroshiku o-negai shimasu* in a business sense. She will be counting on his services as a guide/interpreter, and for this reason as well, *Yoroshiku o-negai shimasu* is appropriate.

This scene is from an animal parody of an *omiai* ("interview" between a prospective bride and bridegroom to let them "look each other over"). Poppo (a common name for a female feline) has just been introduced here. Her mother and father are sitting behind her, and their attire (kimono and pinstripe suit) shows that this is a fairly formal occasion.

© Kobayashi Makoto / *What's Michael?*, Kodansha

<u>Poppo</u>: ポッポ　と　申します。
Poppo to mōshimasu.
"My name is Poppo." (PL4)

よろしく　お願い　します。
Yoroshiku o-negai shimasu.
"Pleased to meet you." (PL3)

- polite cat that she is, Poppo uses the humble word *mōshimasu* when giving her name. *Mōshimasu* would be considered very polite speech (PL4), but she still uses *o-negai shimasu* (ordinary polite — PL3), instead of the very polite *o-negai itashimasu* (PL4).
- compare her choice of words with that of her male counterpart on the next page.

More introductions

The male half of this *omiai* is a dog, who uses more informal speech. Although his speech is certainly socially acceptable (for a male), it would not be strange for a young man to say *Yoroshiku o-negai shimasu* in this situation.

© Kobayashi Makoto / *What's Michael?,* Kodansha

Shinnosuke: 伸之助　です。
Shinnosuke desu.
"I'm Shinnosuke." (PL3)

よろしく...
Yoroshiku...
(This is where the translating gets tough. His casual tone is something like **"Hi, I'm Shinnosuke,"** but because *yoroshiku* is in itself a rather polite word, it could be **"I'm Shinnosuke, my pleasure . . ."**).

• his choice of words is part of the image of this cartoon character—he is wearing a loud sports coat, and behaves in a good-natured but somewhat rough manner. The conclusion of this *omiai* was that the pair were not compatible.

This young man is introducing his bride-to-be to his aunt. By simply using the (humble) word *itashimasu* instead of *shimasu*, she has increased the politeness level of her speech. Note that *itashimasu* is used only for one's own actions, not those of other people.

© Yajima & Hirokane / *Ningen Kōsaten*, Shogakukan

Yōko: 大川　容子 です。
Ōkawa Yōko desu.
"I'm Ōkawa Yōko."

今度　　　　宏平さん　と　結婚する　ことになりました。
Kondo　　Kōhei-san　to　kekkon suru　koto ni narimashita.
this time/soon (name-hon.) with　marry　　it has come about that
"(It has come about that) Kōhei and I are to be married." (PL3)

よろしく　お願い　致します。
Yoroshiku o-negai itashimasu.
Given the situation, she would seem to be saying, **"Please accept me as a member of the family and be nice to me."** (PL4)

A new business relationship

This is not an introduction. He has just been promoted to an executive position, and she is his new secretary, but they already know each other as employees of the same company. In this case, *Yoroshiku o-negai shimasu* has a connotation of "Let's cooperate/Let's work together harmoniously." As a female, and as a secretary/subordinate, this woman would almost be bound to use the more polite *itashimasu*.

©Yamasaki & Kitami / *Tsuri-Baka Nisshi*, Shogakukan

Exec: よろしく お願い しますよ、中野さん。
Yoroshiku o-negai shimasu yo, Nakano-san.
(You know what this means by now, right?)

Sec: こちら こそ、よろしく お願い いたします。
Kochira koso, yoroshiku o-negai itashimasu.
"It's me who should say *Yoroshiku ...*" (PL4)

- *yo* after *shimasu* simply adds emphasis, but this would be used among peers or by a superior.
- *kochira koso* means something like "I am the one who should be asking for your kind cooperation/consideration." *Kochira*, (literally "this way/direction") can be used to refer to oneself, or, with a gesture, to someone else.
- *koso* means "indeed/all the more."

New Year's greetings

It's not just women who use polite speech. In these panels, a section chief (課長, *kachō*) is exchanging New Year's greetings with his department head (部長, *buchō*). In the second panel they are both bowing, so we can't see the face of the person speaking. The feeling of this greeting is mutual, but the use of the verb *itashimasu* would indicate that this is the subordinate (section chief) speaking.

©Yamasaki & Kitami / *Tsuri-Baka Nisshi*, Shogakukan

Sec. Chief: ドモ、おめでとう ございます！！
Domo, omedetō gozaimasu!!
"Congratulations!"
→ **"A very Happy New Year!!"** (PL4)

Dept. Head: あ、おめでとう。
A, omedetō.
"Oh, Happy New Year."

- *omedetō* is derived from the adjective *medetai*, meaning "auspicious, joyous." Japanese people congratulate each other on the "dawning" of the new year.

Sec. Chief: 今年 も 昨年 同様 よろしく お願いいたします。
Kotoshi mo, sakunen dōyō, yoroshiku o-negai itashimasu.
this year also last year same manner well/favorably please
"This year, the same as last year, I ask for your kind favor." (PL4)

Setting up the deal

Business talks call for frequent use of *yoroshiku o-negai shimasu* on both sides. In this scene, two Korean businessmen are entertaining the director of a company called Kanemaru Sangyō (Kanemaru Industries). They represent a manufacturing concern and want Kanemaru Sangyō to import and distribute their products.

1st Businessman: ぜひ　　金丸産業さん　に　わが　韓国の　製品　も　取り扱ってもらいたい　と　思いましてね。
Zehi　Kanemaru Sangyō-san ni　waga Kankoku no　seihin　mo　toriatsukatte moraitai　to　omoimashite, ne.
by all means (Co. name- hon.)　by our　Korean　products also　would like to have handled　(quote)　thinking (colloq.)
"We would definitely like to have Kanemaru Sangyō handle our Korean products, too." (PL3)

2nd B'man: なに　と　ぞよろしく。
Nani　to　zo yoroshiku.
"If you would, please give us your favorable consideration." (PL3 - implied)

- note that *-san* has been added to the company name just as if it were a person's name.
- *waga* . . . is a somewhat literary way of saying "our/my."
- . . . *to omoimashite* ("thinking that. . .") on the end sounds much softer and smoother than ending with . . . *desu.*
- the rather formal *nani to zo* can be thought of as "dressing up" *yoroshiku,* which would be a little too informal in this situation. This is somewhat like *Dōzo yoroshiku* in an introduction.

Director: いやあこちらこそよろしく　お願い　しますよっ。
Iyā　kochira koso yoroshiku o-negai shimasu yo!
"No, we are the ones who must ask for your co-operation!" (PL3)

- *iyā* or simply *iya* is a somewhat masculine way of saying "no."
- even though he is being wined and dined, the director realizes that both sides of a business deal need each other.
- the small *tsu* at the end of his sentence indicates an emphasis/intonation that we reflect by using an exclamation mark in the English translation.

© Ueyama Tochi / *Cooking Papa*, Kodansha

Making a payoff

At a political rally, the man on the left (modeled loosely after corrupt political kingpin Kanemaru Shin) shows up to embarrass a rival group. In this scene, an aide from the rival camp offers him an envelope, supposedly filled with money, to get him to stay away.

© Yamasaki & Kitami / *Fuku-chan,* Shogakukan

Aide: これで　よろしく　お願いします
Kore de　yoroshiku o-negai shimasu.
this with well/favorably please
"Let us offer you this for your cooperation."
(PL3)

• the hand-to-the-head gesture indicates embarrassment.

Please take good care of them

This woman is giving away a litter of kittens, and as the recipients leave with their mewing charges, she gives them a *Yoroshiku o-negai shimasu.*

© Kobayashi Makoto / *What's Michael?,* Kodansha

Recipients: それじゃ　たいせつに　そだてます　ので。
Sore ja,　taisetsu ni sodatemasu　no de.
with that carefully (will) bring up so/therefore
"Then, we will bring them up carefully, so . . ."
毎月　　写真　を　とって　送ります。
Maitsuki shashin o totte okurimasu.
every month photo (obj.) take-and send
"We'll take pictures every month and send them." (PL3)

Housewife: よろしく　おねがい　します。
Yoroshiku o-negai shimasu.
"Please take good care of them. / I entrust them to your care." (PL3)

Kittens: ミイーミイー。
Mii–, mii–.
"Mew, mew."

• the first sentence ends in *no de* ("therefore/so") and the implied conclusion would be "don't worry about the kittens/please be reassured."
• her use of *Yoroshiku . . .* implies she is counting on them to take good care of the kittens.

Lesson 2 • *Sumimasen* 済みません

This one versatile expression can be used to express sentiments ranging from "I'm sorry," or "Excuse me" to "Thank you." In the following examples, perhaps you can see a consistent pattern underlying these diverse usages.

This is not the end?

Sumimasen derives from the verb *sumu*, which literally means "end/be concluded/be settled." For example:

> 試験が済みました。
> *Shiken ga sumimashita.*
> "<u>Exams are over.</u>" (PL3)

It's a fairly easy step to the meaning of "get off/escape with..." For example:

> 罰金で済む。
> *Bakkin de sumu.*
> "It ends with a fine." → "<u>Get off with (only) a fine.</u>"

Two other verbs (住む *sumu* = "live/dwell/reside," and 澄む *sumu* = "become clear/translucent") have the same pronunciation, but both have a different kanji and different meaning. Even written as 済む (the kanji associated with *Sumimasen*, "Excuse me/Thank you"), the word has subtle variations in meaning.

The negative form of this verb, 済みません *sumimasen*, could be thought of as meaning "it has not ended/this is not the end." That is, it implies a feeling of indebtedness or a feeling that the situation has not been settled. This could be the result of having committed an offense/impropriety for which one must make amends (*sumimasen* = "excuse me"), or the result of having received a favor which creates a debt (however small) of gratitude (*sumimasen* = "thank you").

   Sumimasen is the PL3 negative form of the verb, but the PL2 negative form, *sumanai*, is sometimes used colloquially, almost exclusively by males. The *-mi-* in *sumimasen* tends to get a light touch, and especially in rapid speech, the word comes out sounding like *suimasen*. There are other more extreme corruptions of the word, for example *suman* (used by males, older people and in some dialects) and *sumanē* — a rough form used only by males, especially gangsters, laborers, and other tough types.

Keeping all this in mind, let's look at some specific *sumimasen* situations.

"Excuse me"

Let's start with some pure "Excuse me" situations. For example, the boss has stopped by for a visit, your cat jumps up on the table, and the result is an embarrassing situation like this.

© Kobayashi Makoto / *What's Michael?*, Kodandsha

Host: おりなさい って ば!!
Orinasai   tte   ba!!
get down   if/when I say
"I said get off the table!!" (PL2)

Cat: ウニャッ
Unya!
"Meow!"

- *orinasai* is a command form of the verb *oriru* (to get/come down). *-Nasai* is a command form of an honorific verb, *nasaru*, so *orinasai* is "nicer" than the abrupt command form, *oriro*. *Orinasai* gives something of the tone of talking to a child.
- *-tte ba* can be thought of as an abbreviation of the phrase *to ieba* ("if [I] say"), so *orinasai tte ba* gives the feeling of "If I say 'Get down,' I mean 'Get down'/You'd better get down." The speaker is showing exasperation because he isn't being listened to.

© Kobayashi Makoto / *What's Michael?*, Kodandsha

Host: まったく もー どうもすみません!!
Mattaku   mō,   Dōmo sumimasen!!
completely already indeed   I'm sorry
"I can't believe this. I'm really sorry!!"
(PL3)

Cat: ウニャニャッ
Unyanya!
"Umeowmeow!"

- *mattaku mō* is an expression of exasperation. The literal meaning of *mattaku* is "completely/utterly," or "truly/indeed." *Mō* literally means "already/now," for example, *mō (iya da na/iya ni natchau)* would mean "That's disagreeable/disgusting (already)."
- the long, squiggly line indicates a drawing out of the *−o* sound.
- *nyā* is the standard cat sound ("meow"). Articulate cat that he is, Michael uses numerous variations of this sound.
- the small *tsu* at the end of Michael's yowl shows a sharp cutting off of the sound. We indicate this with an exclamation mark in the English translation.
- the hand-to-the-head is a standard gesture of embarrassment.

"Excuse me and thank you"

Being embarrassed by your mother seems to have a rather universal nature. This young lady's mother has come to visit her in Tokyo. The mother unabashedly approaches a couple in the park, asks them to take a photo of her with her daughter, and is now in the process of taking their photo to return the favor. The daughter is apologizing for her mother's behavior. Here, the use of *sumimasen* is still very close to the English "excuse me," but there is a hint of "thank you" creeping in, as the girl not only apologizes, but also thanks the couple for playing along with her mother.

Daughter: すみません いなか者 の 母 な もの です から...
Sumimasen. Inakamono no haha na mono desu kara...
I'm sorry bumpkin/rustic (=) mother (adj.) situation is because
"Excuse us. My mother is from the country, so . . ." (PL3)

Passerby: いいえ。
Iie.
no
"Oh, no (That's all right)."

Mother: カズ子!!
Kazuko!!
(name)
"Kazuko!!"

- *inakamono* is a person from the country. *Inaka* = "country/countryside," and *mono* (written with this kanji) means "person."
- the word *haha* is used to refer to your own mother, while someone else's mother is *okāsan*. The daughter would probably call her mother *okāsan* when speaking to family members or friends, or when addressing her mother.

Mother: なに ゴチャゴチャ 言っとる ん ね。
Nani gocha gocha ittoru n ne.
what mish-mash/confusion are saying (explan.) (colloq.)

そこ どきなさい。
Soko dokinasai.
there move aside/away
"What are you mumbling about? Get out of the way." (PL2)

- *gocha gocha* means "(a) mishmash/confusion," and *gocha gocha (o) iu* means "mutter/mumble." In dialects (e.g. Kansai dialect) *oru* is frequently used instead of *iru*, and *ittoru* is a contraction of *itte-oru* (*itte-iru* in "standard Japanese").
- the *n* before *ne* is a contraction of *no*, used here to indicate a question.
- *dokinasai* is a command form of the verb *doku* ("get out of the way/make room for").

Daughter: もう...
Mō...
already
"Really!"

- the daughter uses *mō* in a manner nearly identical to that of the exasperated host in the last example. She is probably thinking *mō iya da* ("This is unpleasant, already/I can't stand it").

"I'm sorry"

At the train station: This man asked the prices of several *obentō* box lunches and has discovered that he doesn't have enough money to buy even the cheapest one. He apologizes and asks for an even cheaper item instead.

こっち　の　一番安い　やつ　は　六百円。
Kotchi no ichiban yasui yatsu wa roppyaku-en.
this direction ('s)　cheapest　one as-for　¥600
"This cheapest one is ¥600." (PL2)

- *kotchi* is a colloquial form of *kochira* = "This way/this place." The particle *no* is necessary in order for this to modify a noun.
- *ichiban yasui* = "cheapest"
- *yatsu* is a slang word which means "guy/fellow," but can be used to mean "thing/one."

あ、すいません。じゃ、菓子パン　と　牛乳 下さい。
A, suimasen. Ja, kashi-pan to gyūnyū kudasai.
Oh　I'm sorry　then sweet bread and　milk　please
"Oh, I'm sorry. Well, sweet bread and milk, please."
(PL3)

- *kashi* means "candy/sweet" or "confection," and *pan* means "bread," so *kashi-pan* is a kind of sweet bread or roll.
- *sumimasen* frequently comes out as *suimasen*.
- again, the hand to the head is used as a gesture of embarrassment.

© Yajima & Hirokane / *Ningen Kōsaten,* Shogakukan

Before asking a favor

***Sumimasen* is a good** way to begin if you're asking someone a favor. For example, asking someone to let you ahead of them in line at a taxi stand.

© Tanaka Hiroshi / *Naku-na Tanaka-kun,* Take Shobo

Man A: すみません、先 を ゆずってください。
Sumimasen, saki o yuzutte kudasai.
excuse me priority (obj.) please yield/concede
"Excuse me, could I go ahead of you?" (PL3)

Man B: 順番 を 守れ よ！
Junban o mamore yo!
sequence (obj.) maintain/guard (emph.)
"Wait your turn!" (PL2-1)

- *yuzutte* is a form of the verb *yuzuru* = "turn over (to)/transfer," or "give way/concede."
- *saki* has quite a range of meanings — from "point (of a pencil)/tip" to "head/front." In this case, it's probably better to consider the phrase *saki o yuzuru* as a single unit.
- *junban* ="order/turn/sequence."
- *mamore* is the abrupt command form of the verb *mamoru* which can mean "protect," "obey/abide by," or "keep (a promise)."

After receiving a favor

This woman and her boyfriend have borrowed money from the boyfriend's father. *Sumimasen* definitely takes on the tone of "Thank you" here.

© Yajima & Hirokane / *Ningen Kōsaten,* Shogakukan

すみません ね、
Sumimasen ne,
thank you (colloq.)
いろいろ お願い を 聞いていただいて…
iroiro o-negai o kiite itadaite . . .
various requests (obj.) listened to/granted
"Thanks a lot for helping us out so much." (PL3)

- the woman's pose, as well as her style of speaking, suggests too much familiarity and not enough sincerity. The *ne* after *sumimasen* might be appropriate if it were a small favor and a close friend.
- she says *iroiro* ("various") although he really did only one favor — he lent them money.
- *o-negai o kiku* literally means "listen to/hear a request," but it's used to mean "grant a request."
- *itadaite* is the -*te* form of *itadaku* (humble word for "receive"), which shows she's stating the cause/reason for her expression of gratitude. This is a case of "inverted syntax," that is, the normal word order would be . . . *kiite itadaite sumimasen.* Thus, *sumimasen* would determine the politeness level (from a grammatical standpoint).

When served a food or beverage

***Sumimasen* is an appropriate** response when you're served food or beverage. In this example, a young man (Kōsuke from *Dai-Tōkyō Binbō Seikatsu Manyuaru*) is working part time at a restaurant and gets roped into serving tea at a *haiku* competition being held by the owner.

© Maekawa Tsukasa / *Dai-Tōkyō Binbō Seikatsu Manyuaru*, Kodansha

Woman: あっ、すみません。
A! Sumimasen.
"Oh, thank you." (PL3)

Owner: それでは　次、大月さん　まいりましょう。
Sore de wa tsugi, Ōtsuki-san mairimashō.
with that　next　(name-hon.)　let's go (to)
"Then, let's go next to Mr. Ōtsuki." (PL3)

- *sore de wa* can be thought of as "With that/In that case/Well then . . ."
- *mairimashō* is a humble word. In this usage it corresponds in meaning to *ikimashō*.

If someone offers to do a favor

These two friends run into each other at the *sentō* (銭湯, "public bath"), and Kōsuke offers to wash the old man's back. In some *sentō* this service (called *nagashi* 流し) is available from a member of the bath house staff.

© Maekawa Tsukasa / *Dai-Tōkyō Binbō Seikatsu Manyuaru*, Kodansha

Kōsuke: 背中　流しましょー　か?
Senaka nagashimashō ka?
back　shall wash off　(?)
"Shall I wash your back for you?" (PL3)

Old Man: おっすまねえ。
O!, sumanē.
"Oh, thanks." (PL2-1)

- *senaka* = "(a person's) back"
- *nagashimashō* is from the versatile verb *nagasu* which can mean "let (water) flow/flush," or "wash away/scrub."
- in masculine slang speech (especially that of gangsters, laborers, etc.) the vowel combination *ai* can become *ē*. So, *sumanē* is a corruption of *sumanai*, the PL2 version of *sumimasen*. This man is a plumber by trade, and is speaking to someone 40 or so years younger, so this form seems natural, but it's difficult for non-native speakers to use this type of speech.

Lesson 3 • Feminine Speech

Some of the differences between masculine and feminine Japanese are matters of degree, such as the extent of use of "polite" speech forms, but some Japanese words are by their very nature masculine or feminine.

It's good for students of Japanese to know something about feminine speech because:
1) It sounds very unnatural, even ludicrous, for a man to use feminine speech. It could also be taken as an indication that he was not a "serious" student, but was just picking up Japanese from a Japanese girlfriend.
2) A Western woman would not sound completely natural speaking Japanese if she avoided feminine speech altogether. This might be more noticeable in informal situations, but even in formal or business situations there is room for feminine language.
3) It's enjoyable.

Some Specific Points

Women speak in a higher register and use more inflection in their speech. This is obviously not unique to Japanese. Perhaps this similarity to English inflection is why beginning students seem to find the speech of Japanese women easier to understand than that of men. To Western ears, Japanese men tend to speak in more of a monotone, which can be difficult to understand.

Women use more polite speech in more situations. This is not simply out of deference to men, since even women talking with women tend to use feminine (sometimes "more polite") speech. One example is the use of the sometimes honorific, sometimes just "nice/polite" prefix *o-*. Although it's not the common practice, a woman could refer to a meat dish as *o-niku*, (and perhaps avoid some of the "flesh" connotations of *niku* = "meat"). It's not inconceivable that a man would say *o-niku* in a very formal situation, or perhaps to a child, but a woman would be much more likely to use this word. The same could be said for *o-sakana* ("fish"). Words like *o-sushi* and *o-soba* still have something of a feminine touch, but we're getting closer to neutral ground. *O-cha* and *o-furo* are words that generally get the honorific prefix from both men and women.

Women use words which are considered intrinsically feminine. For example:

• *wa* (as an ending) — even this most distinctive of all feminine words is sometimes used by men in Kansai dialect. It's hard to imagine a man, however, using the variations *wa yo*, and *wa ne*.

• the ending *na no*, and perhaps to a somewhat lesser extent, *no yo*.

• *no* (as an ending) — in informal speech, this is more a matter of degree, but using *no* after PL3 *-masu/desu* speech has a decidedly feminine touch.

• *kashira* — used by women to mean "I wonder . . ."

Specific Points (continued)

- *ara* — an expression of surprise which is occasionally used by some males, but has a decidedly feminine tone.

- *mā* — this word can be used in a number of ways, some of which are neutral. The combination *ara mā*, however, has a very feminine touch.

- *atashi* — this softer version of *watashi* ("I/me") is used mostly by women. An even more extreme version is *atai,* which has a little-girl-like quality.

- *chōdai,* as an informal substitute for *kudasai,* has a feminine touch, although it's not so uncommon for a man to use this word (which, unlike *kudasai,* is actually a noun, although idiomatically used as a verb).

In order to be "cute" and perhaps unthreatening, many Japanese girls elongate certain vowel sounds in a style commonly associated with young announcers/commentators (especially females) on radio and television.

Two young OLs

Just between us girls: these two frames could be considered typical informal feminine Japanese. They are from the popular 4-frame series OL 進化論 (*OL Shinkaron,* "Evolution of the OL"). OL stands for "Office Lady."

© Akizuki Risu / *OL Shinkaron,* Kodansha

1st OL: あした　友だち　の　結婚式　なの。
Ashita tomodachi no kekkon-shiki na no.
tomorrow friend 's wedding ceremony is-(explan.)
"Tomorrow is my friend's wedding." (PL2)

2nd OL: へー
Hē
(tone is like "Is that so/you don't say")

- a male might say . . . *kekkon-shiki nan da.*

1st OL: なんだかんだ　お金　が　かかる　でしょ。
Nanda kanda o-kane ga kakaru desho.
this-and-that money (subj.) is required isn't it
"It takes money for this and that." (PL3-2)

月末　なのに　やんなっちゃう　わー。
Getsumatsu na no ni, ya n natchau wā.
end-of-month even-though-it-is becomes unpleasant (fem.)
"Just at the end of the month, what a bummer." (PL2)

- shortening *deshō* to *desho* is not necessarily feminine — but a male would probably use *da rō* in this situation.
- *na no ni* here simply means "even though it's . . ." This is not feminine speech.
- *ya n natchau* is a colloquial form of the expression *iya ni naru.* Literally, *iya* = "disagreeable/unpleasant" and *naru* = "become," so *iya ni naru* means "become unpleasant." *Natchau* is an emphatic version of the verb *naru.*

Feminine but firm

This woman is mildly annoyed because her cat, Michael, has not been very cooperative with the vet. She is telling him in a firm tone (note the hands on the hips) that it's over and they are going home. He obliges by scurrying into the carrying case.

Woman: 終わった わよ、 マイケル。
Owatta   wa yo,   Maikeru
is over   (fem. emph.)   (name)
"It's over, Michael." (PL2)

帰る   わよ!!
Kaeru   wa yo!!
will go home   (fem. emph.)
"We're going home!!"

FX: サァッ
Sā!
(a quick, sudden effect, as in *satto kago ni hairu,* "Rush into the cage").

• Michael was hiding under her blouse in the first panel.

© Kobayashi Makoto / *What's Michael?,* Kodansha

Still a lady

She was about to feed her cats when the phone rang. Now they are starting to bug her, meowing and pawing at her feet. She's losing her temper, but is still using feminine speech forms. When a woman becomes extremely angry and uses masculine speech, the effect is dramatic.

Woman: うるさい わ ねー。
Urusai   wa   nē
bothersome (fem.)(colloq.)
"Shut up!" (PL2)

静かにしてて   よ   もー!!
Shizuka ni shite-te yo,   mo–!!
be quiet-(please)   (emph.)(already)
"Be quiet already!!" (PL2)

• *urusai* is an adjective meaning "noisy/bothersome." A man might say *urusai nā/zo* in this kind of situation.
• *shizuka* can mean "quiet," or "still."
• *shizuka ni shite-(i)te* is a form of *shizuka ni suru* = "be quiet." *Shizuka ni shite-te kudasai* would be more "polite," but if you're talking to your cats, to a close friend or family member, or to a subordinate, you can get away with substituting *yo* for *kudasai.*
• implied after *mō* is something like *mō, iya ni natchau* (see first example).

© Kobayashi Makoto / *What's Michael?,* Kodansha

A slightly elegant touch

The woman being interviewed is a popular "beautiful actress" *(bijin joyū)* who lives in an elegant house and generally has a refined, feminine air. Her pet, however, is Catherine, sometimes known as Nyazilla *(Nyajira)*.

Actress: じつ　は　ね、
Jitsu　wa　ne,
reality　as-for (colloq.)

カトリーヌ　は　踊る　んです　のよ!
Katoriinu　wa　odoru　n desu　no yo!
(name)　as-for dances (explan.)-is (fem.-emph.)
"Actually, Catherine dances!" (PL3)

Interviewer: えー!?　ほんと　です　かー?
E!?　Honto desu kā?
(exclam.)　truth　is　(?)
"Does she really?" (PL3)

- it's the *no* after *desu* (PL3) that makes this sound very soft and feminine.

© Kobayashi Makoto / *What's Michael?*, Kodansha

Does she read his mind?

Not exactly an "item," but not completely platonic, these two are Hiroko and Kōsuke from *Dai-Tōkyō Binbō Seikatsu Manyuaru.*

Kōsuke: 焼きイモ屋　って
Yaki-imo-ya　tte
yaki-imo vendors as-for

夏　の　間　何　してる　の　かな...?
natsu　no aida, nani shite-ru　no　ka na...?
summer　's interval what are doing (explan.) I wonder
(thinking) **"I wonder what *yaki-imo* vendors do during the summer... ?"** (PL2)

- *yaki-imo* is a roast sweet potato sold by street vendors during the cold and cool months of the year. The ending *ya* indicates a person (or a shop) engaged in a particular trade.
- *tte* has the same function as *wa*, or you can think of it as a very contracted form of *to iu no wa.*

Hiroko: 焼きイモ屋さん　て
Yaki-imo-ya-san　te
yaki-imo vendors-(hon.) as-for

夏になる　と　何　してる　の　かしら　ね?
natsu ni naru　to nani shite-ru　no　kashira　ne?
becomes summer when what are doing (explan.) I wonder (colloq.)
"I wonder what *yaki-imo* vendors do when it turns to summer." (PL2)

Kōsuke: え!?　うん... そーだ　ね...
E!?　un... sō da　ne...
(exclam.)　yeah　that's so (colloq.)
"Huh!? uhm . . . well, let's see . . ." (PL2)

- she has added the honorific/polite *-san* to *yaki-imo-ya.*
- as this example illustrates, *kashira* is the feminine equivalent of *ka nā/ka na*. Females sometimes use *ka nā/ka na* when talking to themselves or to close friends, and it's not unheard of for a man to use *kashira*, although this is not going to give a very macho image.

© Maekawa Tsukasa / *Dai-Tōkyō Binbō Seikatsu Manyuaru*, Kodansha

Thinking in masculine speech

When thinking or speaking to themselves, women often revert to plain/abrupt forms that would normally sound masculine. Hiroko bought a wind-chime (風鈴 *fūrin*) for Kōsuke's room, but discovers that he already has one. She is alone in this scene, and the bubbles from the balloon show she is thinking. If someone else were present, she might speak the same line, as if thinking aloud.

Hiroko: あった の か...
Atta no ka...
existed (explan.) (?)
"So he had one . . ." (PL2)

- *atta* is the plain/abrupt past form of the verb *aru* = "there is (for inanimate objects)." So, in a literal sense she is saying "There was one. . ."

© Maekawa Tsukasa / *Dai-Tōkyō Binbō Seikatsu Manyuaru,* Kodansha

A feminine expression of "surprise"

Dressing up for a wedding, Kōsuke shows Hiroko his father's custom-tailored, cashmere coat, which has been passed on to him. Kōsuke seems to think highly of the coat, but checks the "fashion" aspect with Hiroko.

Kōsuke: 古くさい かな？
Furukusai ka na?
old-fashioned I wonder
"I wonder if it's (too) old-fashioned?" (PL2)

Hiroko: アラ かえって 新鮮 よ！
Ara, kaette shinsen yo!
(exclam.) to-the-contrary fresh (emph.)
"Oh, to the contrary, it actually looks fresh!" (PL2)

- if he were thinking to himself, he would probably use the same "words."
- this use of *ara* is like a feigned surprise.
- *kaette* means "contrary to what one might think or expect . . .," or, in this case, "contrary to what you fear . . ."

© Maekawa Tsukasa / *Dai-Tōkyō Binbō Seikatsu Manyuaru,* Kodansha

TV Announcerette "cute"

We don't know where it first started, but this style of elongating certain vowel sounds in a somewhat child-like manner is associated with a type of (usually) female TV "talent." These "announcerettes" seem to be appreciated more for their cute and entertaining qualities than for their intellect.

© Kobayashi Makoto / *What's Michael?*, Kodansha

Announcer: はーい。ここ は 猫 の 惑星 でーす。
Hāi. *Koko wa Neko no Wakusei dēsu.*
yes here as-for cat 's planet is
"Hello! This is the Planet of the Cats." (PL3)

- the program started with a studio announcer, and now she is taking over on location, thus the *hai*.
- the movie "Planet of the Apes" was called *Saru no Wakusei* in Japan. This is a parody featured in *What's Michael*.

Announcer: わあー。かーわいいーん!!
Wā, *kāwaii-n!!*
(exclam.) cute
"Ooh, they're so cuuute!!" (PL2)

- in this scene, she is looking at some very cute cats.
- *Wā* used this way at the beginning is not necessarily feminine speech. It's essentially like "Wow!" — an expression of surprise or amazement used by men and women.
- the *ka* in *kāwaii* has been elongated to stress the word, like "so cuuute!"
- the *n* at the end of *kawaii-n* is not really pronounced. It indicates that the sound is drawn out and ended with a kind of nasal, almost whining tone.

© Kobayashi Makoto / *What's Michael?*, Kodansha

A final note

Our examples came from *OL Shinkaron* (drawn by a woman, Akizuki Risu), from *What's Michael* (drawn by a man, Kobayashi Makoto), and from *Dai-Tōkyō Binbō Seikatsu Manyuaru* (drawn by a man, Maekawa Tsukasa). Although these manga all first appeared in magazines which are primarily targeted at men, the *tankōbon* (collections in book form) are popular with women as well (especially *What's Michael*).

漫

Lesson 4 • *Gaijin* Bloopers

Potential Pitfalls for the Non-native speaker of Japanese

Anyone who has learned a foreign language usually has an amusing anecdote (if not a horror story) to tell about language mistakes. In the interest of promoting Japanese language education, and in the spirit of good clean fun, let's take a closer look at some of the bloopers that have already been made.

Part I: A Reasonably Serious Look

by Karen Sandness

After several years of teaching Japanese at college level, I've begun to form hypotheses concerning the predictable patterns which can be detected in errors made by students of Japanese. These patterns suggest that some types of errors are the result of underlying attitudes or misconceptions.

One attitude which seems to be present in some students at a very deep, subconscious level is *"If It's Good Enough For English, It's Good Enough For Japanese."* These students take English as the norm and have difficulty recognizing distinctions that do not occur in English. In a first-year class, this usually manifests first as problems in pronunciation. Virtually all beginners have some trouble with pronunciation, but the *IIGEFEIGEFJ* learner remains oblivious to such basic distinctions as *su* versus *tsu,* or long vowels versus short vowels, and continues to have pronunciation problems long after his or her classmates have moved on to having problems with the distinction between *-tara* and *-eba.* Such a student might say, *Boku no shumi wa suri desu* (僕の趣味はすりです, "My hobby is pickpocketing") when actually his hobby is fishing (釣, *tsuri*).

The students whose *IIGEFEIGEFJ* attitude extends to grammar are even more creative with their bloopers. They may do just fine in drill sessions, but when turned loose, they come out with utterances such as *Watashi ikimashita e kōen kinō.* I sometimes get the impression that deep down, they believe that English word order is divinely ordained and that the Japanese would use it if they were just more enlightened.

What is a Blooper?

「ブルーパー」とは要するに、馬鹿げた失敗,「ドジ、ヘマ」に捉えられるような行為だが、そこには「おかしさ」が伴っている。ブルーパーは見る者、聞く者を笑わせ、楽しくさせるものである。最近、日本でもスポーツの失敗シーンなどを多く特集し放送し初めているが、アメリカではかなり以前から人気がある。代表的なものとして、Ed McMahon（エド•マクマーン/The Tonight Show）とDick Clark（ディック•クラーク/American Bandstand）がホストのTV Bloopers and Practical Jokes という人気番組がある。

Next is the ***"This Language Makes No Sense Anyway"*** group. They at least realize that Japanese does not operate as English does, but they perceive Japanese grammar as being completely random in nature. They select particles as much to maintain the rhythm of the sentence as to serve any grammatical function. This leads to such whimsical statements as *Sumisu-san wa hanbāgā ga tabemashita* (sounds like a hamburger ate Smithsan) and *Taitei enpitsu ni kakimasu* (illustration on the right).

TLMNSA types believe that all Japanese verbs and adjectives are irregular. When writing, they evidently flip coins to decide whether they will spell a given *-te* form with *-te* or *-tte*. In the midst of a drill on adjective or verb forms, they call out wild guesses, particularly if the previous line of the drill has just presented an analogous form:

Instructor: *Takai desu ka.*
Reasonably alert student: *Iie, takaku nai desu.*
Instructor: *Nagai desu ka.*
TLMNSA student: *Iie, nagaiku desu.*
Instructor: *Iie, chigaimasu.*
TLMNSA student: *Nagai nai deshita?*
Instructor: *Iie.*
TLMNSA student: *Nagaikatta arimasen no deshita?*

You get the idea. The final manifestation of the ***TLMNSA*** syndrome is the agonized look of foreboding that comes over the student's face whenever he or she is expected to comprehend the spoken language. The student's mind is so filled with thoughts of "I'll never understand this. This makes no sense. Why does she talk so fast?" that Japanese is completely shut out.

I first observed the ***Dictionary Dependence*** phenomenon several years ago when I asked my students to prepare a description of their roommates. One young man announced *Boku no*

Taitei enpitsu ni kakimasu.

rūmumēto wa ana o akeru desu which, if anything, means "My roommate opens holes." When I asked him what he was trying to say, he gave me a snide look and explained, as if to someone who was not very bright, "My roommate is a <u>bore.</u>"

In another instance, a student hurriedly leafed through her pocket dictionary and came up with the statement *Hawai wa Nihon yori shimeru desu.* She thought she was saying, "Hawaii is closer than Japan," but she had picked out the verb "close" as in "close the door," rather than the adjective "close" as in "nearby."

The best way to avoid ***Dictionary Dependence*** bloopers is never to use a Japanese word gleaned from a dictionary unless you have either looked it up again in the Japanese-English section to determine its nuances or asked a Japanese person whether this is in fact the word you are looking for.

Finally, there is the ***Good Enough*** attitude. This sometimes appears in returned exchange students who have learned a slangy, overly informal, and error-ridden variety of Japanese. Their pronunciation, intonation, and self-confidence in speaking are enviable, but too many of them are immune to further polishing. They try to coast through their college Japanese courses, and when the instructor points out grammatical errors or nonstandard usage, they shrug the advice off, evidently figuring that their Japanese was ***"Good Enough"*** for surviving and even thriving in Japan, so why work so hard? These students rarely make further progress.

Another variety of ***"Good Enough"*** can be observed among long-term foreign residents of Japan who after ten or more years in the country know an amount of Japanese comparable to the first page or two of a tourists' phrasebook. They are fond of telling newcomers that it is not necessary to learn more than a few

(continued on p. 41)

Boku no rūmumēto wa ana o akeru desu.

Lesson 5 • *Hiragana, Katakana & Manga*

Written Japanese looks pretty imposing, but the two phonetic "alphabets" (strictly speaking called "syllabaries"), *hiragana* and *katakana*, are fairly easy to learn. Even if your interest in Japanese is only casual, we recommend that you at least become familiar with hiragana and katakana (known collectively as *kana)*. This relatively small investment of time can greatly enhance your enjoyment of manga, and can give you insights into the structure of the spoken as well as written Japanese language.

Speaking of the written language . . .

Since the written language is only a way of representing the system of sounds that make up spoken Japanese, let's begin by taking a look at that system. Below is a chart of the *gojū-on* (五十音 "fifty sounds") which are the basis of the Japanese language. There are some additional variations and combinations, but these are the basic units. (Starting at the top left, read top to bottom, left to right.)

a	ka	sa	ta	na	ha	ma	ya	ra	wa	n
i	ki	shi	chi	ni	hi	mi		ri		
u	ku	su	tsu	nu	fu	mu	yu	ru		
e	ke	se	te	ne	he	me		re		
o	ko	so	to	no	ho	mo	yo	ro	(w)o	

You'll notice these are written using English letters (called *rōmaji* ローマ字, literally "Roman letters"). This is a workable system, although most Japanese people (as well as non-Japanese who are proficient at reading and writing Japanese) find it clumsy to read or write Japanese words in rōmaji.

Now, look at the same chart written in hiragana — the Japanese phonetic "alphabet" which Japanese schoolchildren learn first.

あ	か	さ	た	な	は	ま	や	ら	わ	ん
い	き	し	ち	に	ひ	み		り		
う	く	す	つ	ぬ	ふ	む	ゆ	る		
え	け	せ	て	ね	へ	め		れ		
お	こ	そ	と	の	ほ	も	よ	ろ	を	

One major difference is that Japanese uses a single "letter" or character to represent what is, in most cases, written with two English letters. So we can say that, on a per-character basis, written Japanese is more "compact" than English. This compactness becomes extreme when *kanji* ("Chinese characters") are included.

You've probably also noticed that there are only 46 sounds. Some of the sounds (characters/letters, if you prefer) were dropped along the way, but the name *gojū-on* ("fifty sounds") stuck.

It starts with hiragana

Japanese schoolchildren start with hiragana, which can be considered a kind of "default" writing system — if there is no *kanji* (Chinese character) for a word, if there is a kanji but the writer chooses not to use it (for aesthetic reasons, or because he/she does not remember the kanji), or if the word is not in a special category (foreign words, animal sounds, word to be emphasized, etc.), it is written in hiragana. The verb endings which change to indicate time, positive vs. negative, and probability are written with hiragana. Hiragana can be used to give the correct reading/pronunciation for kanji which may be unfamiliar to the reader. In fact, Japanese can be written entirely in hiragana.

Books for small children are usually written entirely in hiragana. The example below is from a book for 3-year-olds called *O-ekaki O-keiko* (おえかきおけいこ, "Drawing Practice" — the "polite" prefix *o-* gets heavy use in language directed at children). It is part of a series, *Zunō Kaihatsu Shiriizu* (頭脳開発シリーズ, "Brain Developer Series"), from Gakken, Tokyo. (Shown 50% actual size.)

がつ	にち	なまえ		シール
gatsu	*nichi*	*namae*		*shiiru*
month	**day**	**name**		**seal** → **sticker**

てんてん を せん で つなぎましょう。
Tenten　o　sen　de　tsunagimashō.
dots　(obj.)　line　with　let's connect
Let's connect the dots with a line.

なに が でてくる でしょう。
Nani　ga　dete kuru　deshō.
what　(subj.)　come out　probably will
What do you think will appear?

てん と てん は きれいにつないで ね。
Ten　to　ten　wa　kirei-ni　tsunaide　ne.
dot　and　dot　as-for　neatly　connect-(please)(colloq.)
Connect each dot neatly now.

おわったら、すきな いろ をぬりましょう。
Owattara,　suki-na　iro　o　nurimashō.
when finish　liked　color(s)(obj.)　let's paint
When you finish, color it with your favorite colors.

- *tsunagimashō* and *tsunaide* are forms of the verb *tsunagu* = "connect."
- *ne* with the *-te* or *-de* form of a verb is an informal way of making a request, but when directed to a child, it takes on more of the tone of a gentle command.
- likewise, although *-mashō* verb endings are typically translated as "let's —," the English equivalent of these sentences would most likely use the command form ("Connect the dots with a line.")
- *kirei-ni* can mean "neatly" or "prettily," here the former.
- *suki-na iro* means "colors you like/favorite colors."

てんてんを せんで つなぎましょう。なにが でて
くるでしょう。てんと てんは きれいに つないでね。
おわったら、すきな いろを ぬりましょう。

© *O-ekaki O-keiko*, Gakken

Learn with your hands!

Learning to read hiragana is good, but you'll remember it better if you learn to write as well. If you don't want your handwriting to be immediately identifiable as that of a *gaijin*, it's absolutely essential that you pay attention to the order of the strokes. There are workbooks that show you this order and provide space to practice, but as a quick guide the following chart is convenient.

The chart below shows the stroke order for writing each hiragana character, arranged in the standard tables:

- **a** あ, **i** い, **u** う, **e** え, **o** お
- **ka** か, **ki** き, **ku** く, **ke** け, **ko** こ
- **sa** さ, **shi** し, **su** す, **se** せ, **so** そ
- **ta** た, **chi** ち, **tsu** つ, **te** て, **to** と
- **na** な, **ni** に, **nu** ぬ, **ne** ね, **no** の
- **ha** は, **hi** ひ, **fu** ふ, **he** へ, **ho** ほ
- **ma** ま, **mi** み, **mu** む, **me** め, **mo** も
- **ya** や, **yu** ゆ, **yo** よ
- **ra** ら, **ri** り, **ru** る, **re** れ, **ro** ろ
- **wa** わ, **o** を, **n** ん

While we're at it . . .

This is katakana. You'll notice that it is just another way of representing the same *gojū-on* system of sounds. Some of the hiragana and katakana characters even look alike.

Katakana is used to write foreign words phonetically in Japanese, so it's something like italics in English. In manga, sound effects are generally written in katakana, and katakana is frequently used in a somewhat arbitrary way to emphasize a word or to indicate that it is not being used in its conventional sense.

a	i	u	e	o
ア	イ	ウ	エ	オ

ka	ki	ku	ke	ko
カ	キ	ク	ケ	コ

sa	shi	su	se	so
サ	シ	ス	セ	ソ

ta	chi	tsu	te	to
タ	チ	ツ	テ	ト

na	ni	nu	ne	no
ナ	ニ	ヌ	ネ	ノ

ha	hi	fu	he	ho
ハ	ヒ	フ	ヘ	ホ

ma	mi	mu	me	mo
マ	ミ	ム	メ	モ

ya	yu	yo
ヤ	ユ	ヨ

ra	ri	ru	re	ro
ラ	リ	ル	レ	ロ

wa	o	n
ワ	ヲ	ン

Hiragana vs. katakana in manga

This example is from the popular children's manga *Anpan-man*. Even the name *Anpan-man* shows how the use of hiragana and katakana is somewhat arbitrary. The *an* in *anpan-man* refers to a sweetened bean paste or "bean jam" (actually not as unpalatable as it might sound, and still fairly popular in Japan).

An あん is a Japanese word, and there is a kanji available (餡), but it is not one of the kanji recommended for general use by the Ministry of Education. Thus, *an* would "normally" be written in hiragana. One of the most popular ways to eat *an*, however, is in the form of *anpan* — a roll filled with *an* paste, something like a filled doughnut. (*Anpan-man*'s head is shaped like an *anpan* roll.) *Pan* パン is the word for "bread," but this is taken from Portuguese, and thus is usually written in katakana. When the two are written together — *anpan* — there seems to be a tendency to write the entire word in katakana, or at least that's the way *Anpan-man* is written: アンパンマン.

Of course, *Anpan-man* is actually a combination of three words. The *-man* comes from English, and so this too would usually be written in katakana. So, with two out of three of the components of this word being katakana, it's not surprising that the entire word is written in katakana for this cartoon character.

Even the katakana in *Anpan-man* has readings given in hiragana. As we mentioned earlier, Japanese children learn hiragana first, so when katakana is used in this manga, the readings are given alongside in hiragana.

Perhaps for the same reason, the names of the other characters are written entirely in hiragana even though they end in *-man*, which, being from English, would usually be written in katakana.

© Yanase Takashi & Furēberu Kan•TMS•NTV, *Anpan-man*, Shogakukan

<u>Dog:</u> ワンワンワンワン
Wan wan wan wan
"Bow wow wow wow."

<u>Anpan-man:</u> ええー、てんどんまん の おっかさん が、ばいきんまん に...
Ee, Tendon-man no okkasan ga, Baikin-man ni...
what? (name) ('s) Mom (subj.) (name) by
"What? Tendon-man's mother . . . by Germ-man . . ."

- *tendon* is <u>tenpura</u> <u>donburi</u>, *tenpura* on top of a bowl of rice — a favorite with children. This series features an amazing assortment of *-man* characters.
- *okkasan* is a slangy word for "Mom."
- *baikin* = "germ/bacteria"

There is a tendency to write manga sound effects in katakana, even if the effect is a Japanese word, or part of a Japanese word, which could be written in hiragana. This depends somewhat on the individual artist. For example, the sound effects in *What's Michael?* (Kobayashi Makoto) are written almost exclusively in katakana, while *Dai-Tōkyō Binbō Seikatsu Manyuaru* (Maekawa Tsukasa) uses more of a mixture of katakana and hiragana. In some cases the choice of hiragana *vs.* katakana seems to be based on some kind of logic or perhaps aesthetic considerations.

The frames below show Kōsuke, the central figure in *Dai-Tōkyō Binbō Seikatsu Manyuaru,* jumping into a pool and then gliding through the water. In the first frame, katakana is used for the "splash" sound, but hiragana is used for the effect of gliding smoothly through the water.

© Maekawa Tsukasa / *Dai-Tōkyō Binbō Seikatsu Manyuaru,* Kodansha

<u>**Sound FX:**</u> バシャ
Basha
Splash

• this (relatively) loud, percussive effect is written in katakana.

<u>**"Sound" FX:**</u> すー
Sū
(effect of gliding smoothly through the water)

• this soft, smooth effect is written in hiragana.
• we put the second "Sound" in quotes, because it's really just the effect of a smooth motion — gliding through the water doesn't make a sound.

The angular shape of katakana does make it seem more appropriate for loud or percussive sounds, while hiragana, with its smoother more rounded shapes, seems more suitable for softer sounds or "smooth" effects.

From an episode of *Dai-Tōkyō Binbō Seikatsu Manyuaru,* here is an interesting combination of hiragana and *katakana*:

<u>**Sound FX:**</u> じゅじゅーじゅっじゅっ
Ju   jū   ju!   ju!
(the sizzling sound of a *tonkatsu,* "pork cutlet," frying in oil is written in hiragana)

<u>**Sound FX:**</u> パチ パチ
Pachi pachi
(the sharp popping sound is written in katakana)

© Maekawa Tsukasa / *Dai-Tōkyō Binbō Seikatsu Manyuaru,* Kodansha

Other uses of katakana

As we mentioned earlier, katakana can be used to emphasize a word or to indicate that it is not used in its conventional sense/meaning. To really appreciate this kind of usage requires some knowledge of kanji. That takes us out of the scope of this article, but having come this far, we'll at least give one example.

The title of the series *Dai-Tōkyō Binbō Seikatsu Manyuaru* is written like this:

大東京
Dai-Tōkyō = Greater Tokyo (in kanji)

ビンボー
Binbō = poverty (in katakana)

生活
Seikatsu = life/living (in kanji)

マニュアル
Manyuaru = manual (in katakana)

Manyuaru is the English word "manual" transposed phonetically into Japanese, so naturally this is written in katakana. But *binbō* is a common Japanese word for which there are perfectly good, readily recognizable kanji (貧乏), approved by the Ministry of Education for everyday usage. Why is *binbō* written in katakana?

The "hero" of *D.T.B.S.M.* is Kōsuke, a young college graduate who has chosen to live a simple "no-frills" lifestyle. He works only part-time jobs, and spends his time reading and enjoying the simple pleasures of life. He uses the word *binbō* to describe this lifestyle, but this is not *binbō* in the conventional sense of the word. In the very first episode of *D.T.B.S.M.* there are banners declaring *Binbō wa fasshon da* (ビンボーはファッションだ, "*Binbō* is [a] fashion"), *Binbō wa shisō da* (ビンボーは思想だ, "*Binbō* is an ideology") — writing the word *binbō* in katakana emphasizes the fact that this is a special case. Katakana is also considered to evoke more of a contemporary feeling, and since the *binbō* in this series is a contemporary type of "poverty," katakana is appropriate for this reason as well.

Recommended reading

We've only scratched the surface here, so for those who want to know more, we recommend the first 60 pages or so of *Kanji & Kana*, by Hadamitzky and Spahn (Charles E. Tuttle Co.). There is information here about the origins and uses of hiragana and katakana, the mysteries of Japanese punctuation, as well as information on the history, form and construction, and writing of kanji.

There are also several workbook-style texts, as well as computer programs, available for learning hiragana and katakana. When you're learning to write, it's probably a good idea to have your progress checked by a native speaker/writer to avoid developing quirks which may not be noticeable to the non-native writer.

(continued from p. 33)

words of Japanese—that will be *"Good Enough"* for meeting daily needs. The *"Good Enough"* types do not realize (or mind) that they are limiting the range of their experience.

Even the most humble and diligent learners, however, are capable of committing typical *gaijin* errors that no native speaker would ever make. Just as a Japanese speaking English may have trouble with the difference between *he* and *she* and may use the wrong article before a noun — mistakes which would be surprising coming from a native speaker — English speakers venturing into Japanese come up with errors unknown among Japanese people.

Perhaps the most common of these is the superfluous *no.* Some students put *no* at the end of everything that describes a noun. Thus he or she says not only *Kodomo no toki* and *byōki no toki* (correct usage), but also *chiisai no toki, Nihon ni kita no toki,* and *wakaranai no toki* . These people are over-exercising their powers of analogy. Both *kodomo no toki* and *byōki no toki*

are indeed correct since *kodomo* and *byōki* are nouns, but *no* is not necessary between a verb or adjective and the noun it describes. (I suspect that informal uses of *no* such as *Itsu Nihon ni irashita no?* or *Kore wa wakaranai no?* might be the cause of some of this confusion.) The correct forms of the above are *chiisai toki, Nihon ni kita toki,* and *wakaranai toki.*

Another common mistake is not conjugating one's adjectives, i.e., saying *takai nai* instead of *takaku nai, takai ni narimashita* instead of *takaku narimashita,* and *takai deshita* instead of *takakatta desu.* While this is admittedly easier than remembering the correct forms, it's just not the way things are done in Japanese.

Of course, each individual learner has his or her own peculiarities, and each year at least one of my students comes up with a mistake I had never imagined anyone would make. Whatever your level of proficiency is right now, whatever your most frequent errors are, you can improve. In fact, you must keep moving forward if you do not want to start slipping back.

Part II: Can You Top This?

In the interest of science, Mangajin has begun compilation and documentation of *gaijin* bloopers. The difficulty of this task is compounded by a general tendency of respondents to try to forget their more memorable bloopers. In some cases bloopers were attributed to third parties, and some respondents requested anonymity. Here are a few of the bloopers we have compiled so far.

- You can't talk about bloopers without mentioning one of the pioneers of Blooperology, Jack Seward. His classic work *Japanese in Action* recounts several third-party bloopers, but we contacted Seward-*sensei* and asked if he could remember making any bloopers himself. He obliged us with the following story.

  "I remember something that happened shortly after I began studying Japanese at the Army Language School, during the war. We had studied the ending -*sō*, which when added to the stem of an adjective means 'seems to be,' or 'appears to be.' I knew how to make the -*sō* form of an adjective, but . . . One afternoon I ran into an instructor and his wife as they were walking across the campus with their newborn infant in a stroller. People call babies 'cute,' but most of them look pretty ugly to me, and when I looked into that stroller I saw a baby that anyone would have called ugly. Intending to say something nice like 'What a cute-looking baby,' I came out with *Akago ga kawaisō desu ne*, which of course means 'The baby is pitiful,' or 'I feel sorry for the baby.' I had correctly added the -*sō* ending to the adjective *kawaii*, meaning 'cute,' but I didn't realize that *kawaisō* is a special case of colloquial usage."

- Next is a blooper reported by Yoshiko Ratliff, an instructor at the Diplomatic Language Services School of Japanese in Washington, D.C.

  "A student was at a *yakitori* (やきとり, bite-sized chunks of chicken on bamboo skewers, grilled over charcoal) shop and wanted to order a

(continued on p. 147)

Lesson 6 • Two Idiomatic Expressions

おはようございます
Ohayō Gozaimasu
"Good Morning"

おめでとうございます
Omedetō Gozaimasu
"Congratulations"
(greeting for birthdays, New Year's, and auspicious occasions in general)

Idioms can be tricky since they are used in ways which may not be obvious from the meanings of the individual words. We hope our manga examples will give you a better feel for how these expressions are actually used.

Gozaimasu — just naturally polite

Both of these expressions use the verb *gozaimasu*, a "polite/formal" word for "be/is." Functionally, *gozaimasu* is the equivalent of less "polite" verbs such as *desu, (de) arimasu,* or even *da,* but it is one of a group of special verbs that are just intrinsically "very polite" (see page 8 "Warning" about politeness levels). In their *-masu* form, these verbs automatically bring a sentence to what we call PL4 (very polite) speech. Even though *gozaimasu* is used idiomatically in these expressions, we still consider them to be PL4.

One of the distinctive characteristics of *gozaimasu* is that certain adjectives change form when used with it. Adjectives ending in *-ai* change *-ai* to *ō*. Adjectives ending in *-ui* change to *-ū*. The ending *-shii* changes to *shū*.

早い	早いです	早ようございます
hayai →	*hayai desu* →	*hayō gozaimasu*
"It's early." (PL2)	"It's early." (PL3)	"It's early." (PL4)
寒い	寒いです	寒うございます
samui →	*samui desu* →	*samū gozaimasu*
"It's cold." (PL2)	"It's cold." (PL3)	"It's cold." (PL4)
めでたい	めでたいです	めでとうございます
medetai →	*medetai desu* →	*medetō gozaimasu*
"It's joyous." (PL2)	"It's joyous." (PL3)	"It's joyous." (PL4)

In our idiomatic expressions, the "polite" prefix *o-* has been added to the PL4 forms, but *ohayō gozaimasu* still looks like a polite way of saying "it's early." As you can see from our manga examples, however, *ohayō gozaimasu* is not used to mean "it is early," but is strictly an idiom used as a greeting in the morning.

On the other hand, *omedetō gozaimasu* is used with much the same meaning as the PL2 word *medetai*. It's saying literally that the situation or occasion is joyous or auspicious (a major difference from the English "congratulations," which is directed at the person). The use of this PL4 form in what is otherwise PL3 or PL2 speech, however, could be considered idiomatic.

With that in mind, let's look at some specific examples.

He's early — she's not

The roll-down shutter outside this *pan-ya* (bread shop) is still not all the way up (indicating that they are not yet officially open for business), so Kōsuke politely gives his morning greetings and asks if it's OK to come in. The woman behind the counter is surprised because he's there so early.

Although the kanji for "early" (早) can be used to write *ohayō gozaimasu* (お早うございます), it's more often than not written in hiragana.

© Maekawa Tsukasa / *Dai-Tōkyō Binbō Seikatsu Manyuaru*, Kodansha

Kōsuke: おはよーございます。 いい っス か?
Ohayō gozaimasu.　　　Ii　ssu ka?
good morning　　　　good/OK　is it?
"Good morning. Is it OK [Can I come in]?"
(PL2-3)

• *ii ssu ka* is a contraction of *Ii desu ka*, used when asking permission. This is a "cheater" PL3, or an informal way of showing a degree of respect.

Woman: アラ、 早い じゃない。
Ara,　　hayai　ja nai.
(exclam.)　early　aren't (you)
"My, aren't (you) early." (PL2)

• *ara* is a feminine expression of surprise.
• *ja nai* is a contraction of *de wa nai* ("is not").
• the subject of *hayai* is not specified, but given the situation, she's saying "you are early" rather than "it (the hour) is early."

How late is it morning?

A difference in perceptions: he has been up and about and feels like the day is well under way, so he greets her with *konnichi wa*. She is hanging out laundry — a task associated with the morning — so she greets him with *ohayō gozaimasu*. We would guess this scene to be around 10:30 AM. Generally 10:30 – 11:00 is considered the cut-off for *ohayō*, although there's obviously room for individual interpretation.

© Yamasaki & Kitami / *Tsuri-Baka Nisshi*, Shogakukan

Sasaki: こんにちは 奥さん!!
Konnichi wa,　Okusan!!
"Good day, ma'am (Mrs. Hamazaki)!!"
(PL3)

Mrs. Hamazaki: あら 佐々木さん、 おはよう ございます。
Ara. Sasaki-san,　ohayō　gozaimasu.
"Oh, Mr. Sasaki, good morning." (PL3-4)

• *okusan*, a word for "wife," is also used to address married women. In Japanese a "title" is often used as the name would be used in English.

Note: the wet laundry is put on poles (at one time these were bamboo) which are placed on the rack in front of her.

Variations on *Ohayō Gozaimasu*

Adding -san, just like a name, is a common variation on several greetings. *Arigatō gozaimasu* is sometimes rendered as *arigato-san*. This is, however, informal speech.

© Maekawa Tsukasa / *Dai-Tōkyō Binbō Seikatsu Manyuaru*, Kodansha

Jogger: おはよーさん。
Ohayō-san.
"G'morning."

Sound FX: カチャカチャ
Kacha kacha
(rattling of bottles on milk truck)

Sound FX: たったっ
Ta! Ta!
(sound of feet hitting the pavement)

Kōsuke: あっ、どーも...
A! Dōmo...
"Ah!" (*Dōmo*, literally "indeed," is an all-purpose greeting/response.)

• the dash after *-yo* and *do* indicates a long vowel — really a katakana device, but often used with hiragana.

A little unconventional, but completely understandable, *hayō ssu* is *ohayō gozaimasu* with the *o*-dropped and *gozaimasu* contracted to *ssu.* In this scene, Hamazaki and his co-workers are staging a *shuntō* ("Spring offensive") to negotiate bonuses. Hamazaki is known for his bad puns and unconventional/creative use of Japanese.

© Yamasaki & Kitami / *Tsuri-Baka Nisshi*, Shogakukan

Hamazaki: はようっス。
Hayō ssu.
(informal/masculine morning greeting)

Salaryman #1: ご苦労さん!!
Gokurō-san!!
(Idiom)**"I appreciate your hard work!!"**

Salaryman #2: 春闘 勝利。
Shuntō shōri.
spring fight victory
(Slogan)**"Victory in the Spring Offensive."**

Salaryman #3: 要求 貫徹!!
Yōkyū kantetsu!!
demands realization
(Slogan) **"Fulfill our demands!!"**

© Takahashi Rumiko / *Urusei Yatsura*, Shogakukan

Mildy macho, *ossu* is simply a combination of the first and last sounds of *ohayō gozaimasu.* It's a favorite of male students.

Student #1: おはよーっ!
Ohayō!

Student #2: おっす!
Ossu!

Omedetō Gozaimasu — Not so idiomatic

As we pointed out earlier, the *ohayō* in *ohayō gozaimasu* retains little of the "original" meaning of *hayai* ("early"), but *omedetō gozaimasu* is used much like a polite/formalized version of the plain/abrupt *medetai*. In this scene from *Kamui Gaiden*, Kamui has decided to stay with the people of a small fishing village. The men of the village, who have great respect for Kamui, are very pleased.

<u>Villager:</u> チビ共　　には　いい　兄貴　　が　　　出来た　し、
Chibi-domo ni wa ii aniki ga dekita shi,
little kids　for　good big-brother (subj.) has been made and
"The little ones have gotten a good big brother, and

サヤカ　には　　　三国一　　の　花婿　　が
Sayaka ni wa Sangoku-ichi no hanamuko ga
(name)　for　best-in-(place name) (=)　groom　(subj.)

見つかった　　な。
mitsukatta na.
has been found (colloq.)
Sayaka has found the best groom in Sangoku. " (PL2)

ハハハ...
Ha ha ha...
"Ha ha ha..."

<u>Villager:</u> めでたいこと　だ。
Medetai koto da.
joyous affair/matter is
"This is a happy event." (PL2)

<u>Voices:</u> ハハハ...
Ha ha ha...
"Ha ha ha..."

© Shirato Sanpei / *Kamui Gaiden*, Shogakukan

On birthdays

To the tune of "Happy Birthday" — although "Happy Birthday" is commonly sung in English, the words *omedetō* and *tanjōbi* can be substituted. For a one-year-old child, the Japanese words somehow seem more appropriate.

<u>**Song:**</u> おめでとう テツオー
Omedetō Tetsuo–
congratulations (name)

おめでとう テツオー
Omedetō Tetsuo–
congratulations (name)

おめでとう 誕生日
Omedetō tanjōbi–
congratulations birthday

(omitted) おめでとう テツオー
Omedetō Tetsuo–
congratulations (name)

© Yajima & Hirokane / *Ningen Kōsaten*, Shogakukan

Today is *Omedetō*

On her wedding day, this man who has been "like a father" brings a gift to the bride at her home, before the party leaves for the ceremony. When he says *omedetō gozaimas*u, he takes the option of specifying the subject and says, literally, "Today is *omedetō*." This illustrates the difference between the Japanese *omedetō* (said of the situation) and the English "congratulations" (said to the person).

© Maekawa Tsukasa / *Dai-Tōkyō Binbō Seikatsu Manyuaru*, Kodansha

<u>**Hide**</u>: あの、本日　は　まことに　おめでとうございます。
Ano, honjitsu wa makoto ni omedetō gozaimasu.
uhh　this day　as-for　indeed　is auspicious
"Eh, today is indeed, (a) joyous (occasion)." (PL4)

- *honjitsu* means "this day," but it also implies "the events of this day."

To the bride, he says "Become happy." This would not be said to the groom since it's now the groom's responsibility to make the bride "happy."

<u>**Man**</u>: お幸せに。
O-shiawase ni.

- the implied complete thought would be something like *O-shiawase ni natte kudasai* ("Please become happy").

© Maekawa Tsukasa / *Dai-Tōkyō Binbō Seikatsu Manyuaru*, Kodansha

Close to "Congratulations"

A woman named Asada (family name) has been promoted to *kachō* (section chief). Her co-workers are applauding the announcement and offering their "congratulations."

<u>**Sound FX**</u>: パチ　パチ　パチ　パチ
Pachi pachi pachi pachi
clap clap clap clap

<u>**Voices**</u>: おめでとうございます、麻田課長!!
Omedetō gozaimasu, Asada-kachō!!
"Congratulations, Asada-kachō!!"

© Torii Kazuyoshi / *Top wa Ore Da!*, Shogakukan

Really just a bad pun

The standard New Year's greeting in Japanese is *Akemashite omedetō gozaimasu*. Note, however, that this is used only after the beginning of the new year. The *akemashite* in this expression is from the verb *akeru* (明ける), which refers to the breaking of dawn or the beginning of a new year/era. It's pronounced the same as another verb (開ける *akeru*), which is a transitive verb meaning "open/unlock." Of course, to make this "pun" possible on paper, *akeru* is written in hiragana.

あけましておめでとう

Title: あけましておめでとう
Akemashite Omedetō
(New Year's greeting, or . . .)

1

Tanaka-kun: あかない なー、このフタ。
Akanai   nā,   kono futa.
doesn't open (colloq.) this   lid
"This lid won't open." (PL2)

"Sound" FX: ギュッ!
Gyu!
(effect of something being squeezed or twisted)

Label: ベンピ(薬)
Benpi (gusuri)
Constipation (medicine)

- *akanai* is the plain/abrupt negative of the verb *aku* ("open/be opened").
- the normal word order would be *kono futa (wa) akanai nā*. This inverted word order is common in colloquial speech.

2

Tanaka-kun: んんー
Nn–
(straining sound)

3

Sound FX: パカッ
Paka!
(sound of tightly closed lid suddenly opening)

Tanaka-kun: あいた!
Aita!
"It opened!" (PL2)

4

Friend: あけまして おめでとー。
Akemashite   omedetō.
"Happy New Year" (or "Congratulations on opening [it].")

Tanaka-kun: そんな 大げさな ことじゃないんだけど なー。
Sonna   ōgesa-na koto ja nai   n da kedo nā.
that kind of exaggerated thing   is not   (expl.) but (colloq.)
"It's not such a big thing." (PL2)

- *ōgesa-na* = "exaggerated/inflated."
- *ja nai* ("is not") actually completes the thought, but adding *da kedo* ("but") leaves the subject open for further comment/counter-comment.

Lesson 7 • Creative Kanji Readings

In Lesson 5 we saw that the hiragana and katakana syllabaries are simply phonetic symbols, that is, they are used to represent sounds, but have no inherent meaning. Kanji, on the other hand, are graphic representations of things or ideas, and most kanji can be read in two or more ways. A writer has the option of specifying or clarifying the reading of a kanji by "spelling it out" phonetically in hiragana or katakana beside the kanji. These readings are called *furigana*. Some writers, especially manga artists, give creative or unconventional furigana to make "puns" or just to make the language more colorful. Here are some examples.

"Cherry," the deranged monk

Takahashi Rumiko, creator of the popular manga *Urusei Yatsura*, is well known for her creative naming of characters and also for her puns. The character "Cherry" is one example.

Shinobu: 錯乱坊 . . .
Cherii . . .
"(It's) Cherry . . ."

Cherry: 海　は　いい　のう!
Umi　wa　ii　nō!
ocean　as-for　nice　isn't it
"I love the ocean!" (PL2)

- using *nō* like the ending *nē* is characteristic of the speech of older people.
- all kanji in the *Urusei Yatsura* series have furigana.

© Takahashi Rumiko / *Urusei Yatsura*, Shogakukan

Takahashi-sensei has given the reading *cherī* (the English word "cherry" written phonetically in katakana チェリー) beside a made-up combination of kanji which looks like it would be read as *sakuranbō*. *Sakuranbo* written 桜んぼ is the Japanese word for "cherry" (the fruit). This character's name, however, is written with the kanji 錯乱 (*sakuran,* "derangement/aberration"), and 坊 (*bō,* [Buddhist] priest").

Cherry is a wandering monk who simply appears from time to time, usually to warn the other characters of impending doom, or to "protect" them. He generally causes more problems than he solves and his preoccupation with the (superficial) supernatural makes this name seem very appropriate.

Mini-Definitions for English words

In this scene, from the beginning of 沈黙の艦隊 (*Chinmoku no Kantai,* literally "The Silent Fleet," but co-titled in English "The Silent Service"), it appears that a submarine has been sunk in an accident, but this man believes it is a trick — that the sub has actually been diverted to another purpose.

© Kawaguchi Kaiji / *Chinmoku no Kantai,* Kodansha

Officer: 擬装... だ な。
Torikku ... da na.
"It's a trick . . . isn't it." (PL2)

- *torikku* is written beside kanji that would normally be read as *gisō*, sometimes translated as "camouflage," but used figuratively to mean "deceptive appearance."
- the English word "trick" is commonly used in Japanese, transliterated into katakana as *torikku*, and we can assume that this character, even though he is Japanese and speaking to another Japanese person, actually said *torikku*. It's as if the kanji were added on to clarify the meaning. In fact, there are other Japanese words which could be used in the sense of "trick," but *gisō* seems appropriate in this situation.

This is an American pilot, responding to a radio communication.

了解。
Rajā.
"Roger."

- *rajā* is written beside the kanji that would normally be read as *ryōkai,* the Japanese equivalent of "roger" in radio communications. If this pilot were Japanese, he would probably have said *ryōkai.*

© Kawaguchi Kaiji / *Chinmoku no Kantai,* Kodansha

On an American ship, there is an announcement that a Mark 46 torpedo has begun homing in on its target.

マーク46　自動追尾　開始!
Māku yonjūroku hōmingu kaishi!
mark 46　　automatic pursuit start
"The Mark 46 has commenced homing!"

- *hōmingu* is written beside kanji that would normally be read *jidō tsuibi,* literally "automatic pursuit."

© Kawaguchi Kaiji / *Chinmoku no Kantai,* Kodansha

The many faces of *hito*

The word *hito* ("person/people/others") is used in a number of ways. It can be used for its vagueness when referring to a member of the opposite sex, especially since using *onna* or *otoko* can sound too blunt/direct. It's also used in some situations where a pronoun ("he/she/them") would probably be used in English.

© Maekawa Tsukasa / *Dai-Tōkyō Binbō Seikatsu Manyuaru*, Kodansha

Friend: きれいな 女 だ な。
Kirei-na hito da na.
pretty person/woman is (colloq.)
"She's pretty, isn't she." (PL2)

Kōsuke: ええ...
Ee...
"Yeah..."

- *hito* is written beside the kanji for *onna* = "woman." Saying *hito* instead of *onna* perhaps implies that he is looking at her more as a person and less as simply a member of the opposite sex.
- it's interesting that *kirei* can also be used to mean "neat/clean/tidy."

On the lookout for a boyfriend for her daughter, this woman (Kyōko's mother from *Mezon Ikkoku*) spots a potential suitor.

© Takahashi Rumiko / *Mezon Ikkoku*, Shogakukan

Woman: あの 男 誰 です?
Ano hito dare desu?
that person/man who is
"Who is he?" (PL3)

Employee: この テニスクラブ の コーチ です よ。
Kono tenisu kurabu no kōchi desu yo.
this tennis club 's coach is (emph.)
"That's the coach of this tennis club." (PL3)

- *hito* is written beside the kanji for *otoko* = "man." In this situation, *ano otoko* would sound a little blunt. The kanji is a bit of information for the reader.
- the word *dare* ("who") makes it clear that this is a question, even though she dropped the *ka* at the end.

© Takahashi Rumiko / *Mezon Ikkoku*, Shogakukan

Meanwhile, the coach is explaining to Kyōko about the other woman she saw him with.

Coach: あの 女 は ただの ゆきずりの...
Ano hito wa tada no yukizuri no...
that person/woman as-for simply passing by
"That was just someone passing by..."
(PL2)

- *hito* is written beside the kanji for *onna* = "woman."

Ishinomori-sensei's use of *hito*

From the series *Hotel*, by Ishinomori Shōtarō, these scenes show *hito* being given as the reading for two different kanji compounds. The word *hito* is also used to refer to "character/personality" (for example *hito ga ii* means "good natured/kindhearted"), and there seems to be something of that implication in these uses.

© Ishinomori Shōtarō / *Hotel*, Shogakukan

Sekikawa: 燃えてる　な、　真理さん!!
Moete-ru   na,   Mari-san!!
is burning (colloq.) (name-hon.)
"Mari is burning up, isn't she!!" (PL2)

Matsuda: あの　　女性　　　が　燃える　と、　コワイよ。
ano   hito   ga moeru to, kowai yo.
that person/woman (subj.) burns if/when scary (emph.)
"When she gets mad, she's frightening . . ." (PL2)

- *hito* is written beside the kanji for *josei* = "female/woman."
- *josei* is more of an objective evaluation of her gender than *onna* might be.
- this is a figurative use of the verb *moeru* ("burn"), but the meaning is obvious.

The guest is impressed that the manager of the hotel (on the left) has come to the lobby to see him off.

© Ishinomori Shōtarō / *Hotel*, Shogakukan

Guest: おやおや。　君　ほど　の　人物　が、
Oya oya.   Kimi hodo no hito ga,
(exclam.)   you extent 's person (subj.)

ロビーで　お見送り　とは　　ねえ!
robii de o-miokuri to wa   nē!
lobby in seeing off the-idea-of (colloq.)
"Well, well, a person like you, seeing (me) off in the lobby . . . !"
(PL indeterminate)

- *hito* is written beside the kanji normally read as *jinbutsu* = "person-age/character."
- *kimi* is an abrupt/familiar word for "you" used almost exclusively by males. Because of his age and status (as a guest), his use of *kimi* seems quite natural — more friendly than condescending.
- ending with *to wa (nē)* implies that the preceding situation is cause for surprise.

Slang readings

In these examples, the furigana readings are slang or colloquial contractions. First from Kobayashi Makoto's *What's Michael* —

© Kobayashi Makoto / *What's Michael?*, Kodansha

Title: Vol. 56:   The 人質
Boryūmu gojūroku: Za   Hitojichi
Vol. 56: The Hostage
刑事山村
Deka Yamamura
Yamamura the Cop

- if pronunciation is limited to the Japanese phonetic system, "The" (in the title) would be pronounced *za*.
- *deka* is written over the kanji for *keiji* = "[police] detective."
- *Yamamura* is the name of the cop.

Sound FX: ウウウウウウ
Uuu uuu
(wailing siren)

Sound FX: ファンファンファン
Fan fan fan
(warning sound from police car)

Colloquial contractions

In spoken Japanese, the word *mono* ("thing/things/products") is frequently contracted to *mon*. In this example from *Mezon Ikkoku,* by Takahashi Rumiko, the reading *mon* is shown beside the kanji for *shinamono* ("merchandise/goods").

© Takahashi Rumiko / *Mezon Ikkoku*, Shogakukan

ビデオ...
Bideo
"A video . . ."
いい 品物　　そろえてやがん　　な...
Ii　 mon　　soroete-yagan　　　na.
nice　thing(s)　have accumulated (derog.)(colloq.)
"You got some nice stuff." (PL1)

- *soroete* is from the verb *soroeru* = "accumulate (a complete set of)"
- *-yagan* is a contraction of *-yagaru*, an insulting form which is used here in a friendly way, but which requires caution.

Another contraction, also from *Mezon Ikkoku.*

© Takahashi Rumiko / *Mezon Ikkoku*, Shogakukan

三鷹　ん　家　に 行く!?
Mitaka　n　chi　ni　iku!?
(name)　's　home　to　go
"You're going to Mitaka's house!?" (PL2)

- *chi* is written beside the kanji for *uchi* — making it immediately clear that *Mitaka n chi* is a contraction of *Mitaka no uchi.*
- Mitaka is a family name.
- using a name this way without an honorific such as *-san* is called *yobisute.*

A touch of old Japanese

From *Kamui Gaiden*, this scene shows fishermen setting out to sea. All of the readings given as furigana are pure/original Japanese words, while the kanji compounds are imports from China. Although the meanings are essentially the same, the pure/original Japanese words are certainly more appropriate in this setting. Although the word *nariwai* is not commonly used now, *iki* and *inochi* are still used in the same sense, especially by those who value tradition, such as sushi chefs.

鮮度　が　生命　の　生業　である。
Iki ga inochi no nariwai de aru.
freshness (subj.) life ('s) livelihood is
"It is a livelihood whose lifeblood is freshness." (PL2)

- *iki* is written above the kanji for *sendo* = "freshness."
- *inochi* is written above the kanji for *seimei* = "life"
- *nariwai* is written above the kanji for *seigyō* = "livelihood."

© Shirato Sanpei / *Kamui Gaiden*, Shogakukan

A reverse twist — *ateji*

Foreign names such as Michael are usually written phonetically in katakana, but by picking kanji with the right sounds, it's possible to write almost any name in kanji. Kanji which are used just for their sound (to write foreign words, etc.) are called *ateji* 当て字 — a combination of *ate* from the verb *ateru* ("assign/allocate to"), and *ji* ("letter/character"). Writing Michael's name in kanji is a humorous way of fitting him into this old setting.

© Kobayashi Makoto / *What's Michael?*, Kodansha

Woman: 舞家瑠　よ、／この　仇　をとっておくれ。
Maikeru yo, / kono kataki o totte okure.
(name) (emph.) / this revenge (obj.) please take
"Michael / please get revenge." (PL3)

Michael: ウニャ？
Unya?
"Meow?"

- *mai* is written with the kanji for "dance," as in the *shishi mai* ("lion dance") which Michael tries (unsuccessfully) to incorporate into his revenge.

Lesson 8 • *Dōmo*, the All-Purpose Word

Dōmo, meaning "indeed/really/quite," is added to a number of expressions to make them more emphatic, but it's also used as a shortened form of those same expressions. It's inherently polite and relatively easy to pronounce, making it an ideal choice if you're at a loss for words.

Thank you

You've probably run into *dōmo* added to *arigatō (gozaimasu)* to make it more emphatic ("Thank you **very much indeed**").

Slightly embarrassed by her mother, who has asked these two strangers to take their picture, this young woman gives a formal "Thank you very much." She's probably also thanking them for humoring her mother. The balloon with three dots coming from her mother probably indicates puzzlement as to why her daughter is being so polite.

© Maekawa Tsukasa / *Dai-Tōkyō Binbō Seikatsu Manyuaru*, Kodansha

Daughter: どうも ありがとう ございました。
Dōmo   arigatō   gozaimashita.
"Thank you so very much." (PL4)

Kōsuke: いえ。
Ie.
"Not at all." (PL2)

Obviously very happy about his new assignment, this young businessman gives a brief but polite "Thank you" as he receives his orders. This is the beauty of the word *dōmo* — it's simple, but still polite. Assigning a politeness level to the single word *dōmo* is a little tricky, but in the scene below we'd be inclined to call it PL3. *Dōmo arigatō gozaimasu* would be PL4.

© Gyū & Kondō / *Eigyō Tenteko Nisshi*, Scholar

Salaryman: どーも。
Dōmo.
"Thank you." (PL3)

- the long dash after *do* makes it into a long *dō*. This is the way vowel sounds are normally elongated in katakana, but using this device with hiragana has something of a pop touch, like the spelling "nite" for "night."

How do you do

Making a cold call on a prospective customer, this young car salesman is announcing his presence by saying *Dōmo hajimemashite*. To make a complete introduction, this would be followed by his company name and his own name. The wavy line after *hajimemashite* shows that he is drawing out this word in something of a sing-song style.

© Torii Kazuyoshi / *Top wa Ore Da!!*, Shogakukan

Salesman: どうも、初めましてー。
Dōmo, hajimemashite–.
"How do you do." (PL3)

Prospect: なんだ、車のセールスマン　か？
Nan da, Kuruma no sērusuman ka?
what is　　car salesman　？
"What's this? A car salesman?"
(PL2)

- *hajimemashite* is like a PL3 *-te* form of the verb *hajimeru* ("begin/start"). Like *hajimete* ("the first time/for the first time"), *hajimemashite* is used as a noun.
- *Nan da* is a very abrupt form of *Nan desu ka* ("What [is it]?"), but it's used as an expression of mild disgust/disappointment, i.e. this is not really a question.

All in their early 20's, these young people are using very short speech forms. In this scene, Hiroko (center) is introducing Kōsuke to her friend, a new-wave type who works in a clothing store in Harajuku. Kōsuke tends to be very succinct in his speech, and he even shortens *dōmo* to simply *domo*.

© Maekawa Tsukasa / *Dai-Tōkyō Binbō Seikatsu Manyuaru*, Kodansha

Friend: 彼氏?
Kareshi?
"Your boyfriend?"

Hiroko: 耕助くん。
Kōsuke-kun.
"Kōsuke."

Kōsuke: ども。
Domo.
"Hi."

- *kareshi,* a word for "boyfriend," is a combination of *kare* ("him") and the ending *-shi,* which is a formal (usually written) version of *-san,* used for adult males, like "Mr."
- calling a male by his first name + *kun* shows a certain degree of familiarity.

Dōmo as a part of formal greetings

Greeting the wife of an old customer, this young salesman uses a polite (PL4) form while the housewife uses PL2.

© Torii Kazuyoshi / *Top wa Ore Da!!*, Shogakukan

Sound FX: カチャ
Kacha
(sound of door opening)

Housewife: あらー、久しぶりねェ、彦野さん。
Arā, hisashiburi nē, Hikono-san.
"My, it's been quite a while, Hikono-san." (PL2)

Hikono: どーも、ご無沙汰 しております。
Dōmo, go-busata shite-orimasu.
"I've really been negligent about calling on you." (PL4)

- *hisashiburi* conveys the meaning of "for the first time in a long time/a long time (since)."
- *busata suru* means "neglect to call on/write to." The *go-* prefix is added even though it's your own *busata*. Using *-orimasu* as an ending instead of *-imasu* is humble speech.

The more polite version of *hisashiburi* includes *de gozaimasu*, the PL4 equivalent of *desu*. *Dōmo* is added for emphasis but doesn't necessarily make it more polite.

Tōdō-san: どうも、お久し振り でございます。
Dōmo, o-hisashiburi de gozaimasu.
"It's been quite a while since I've seen you." (PL4)

© Ishinomori Shōtarō / *Hotel*, Shogakukan

Even if your manners were impeccable, it's considered good form to apologize for your behavior during your previous encounter with someone. In this case, the young salesman actually did commit some breaches of etiquette when he called on this prospect the day before. The prospect did his best to scare the salesman off, so his *yoku kita* indicates surprise that the salesman had the persistence to come back again.

© Torii Kazuyoshi / *Top wa Ore Da!!*, Shogakukan

Prospect: ほー、よく 来た なあ。
Hō, yoku kita nā.
(exclam.) well/persistently came (colloq.)
"Heh, I'm surprised to see you." (PL2)

Salesman: 昨日 は どうも 失礼しました。
Sakujitsu wa dōmo shitsurei shimashita.
yesterday as-for indeed I was impolite
An American might say something like **"Thanks for your time yesterday,"** but this salesman is literally saying **"I was very impolite yesterday."** (PL3)

- *yoku* is the adverb form of *yoi* = "good," and *kita* is the plain/abrupt past form of *kuru* = "come."
- *shitsurei* is a noun meaning "impoliteness," and *shitsurei shimashita* literally means "I was impolite."

Dōmo as an informal greeting

These are car salesmen greeting a customer who has come to a test drive event in which they are promoting a new model. Car salesmen in Japan frequently develop close ties with customers, and these two are using the same kind of informal speech they would use to greet a friend.

© Torii Kazuyoshi / *Top wa Ore Da!!*, Shogakukan

A: おおッ、来た　来たッ!
Ō!　　Kita　　kita!
Oh!　(he) came　(he) came
"Oh! He's here, he's here!" (PL2)

B: やあ、野川さん、どーも!!
Yā,　Nogawa-san,　dōmo!!
"Hey, Nogawa-san, welcome!!" (PL2-3)

- *dōmo* is a handy word for this situation because it can imply any and all of the more formal greetings on the facing page, plus "Thank you for coming to our event," and any other civility which needs to be covered here.

From ***Dai-Tōkyō Binbō Seikatsu Manyuaru,*** Kōsuke and Hiroko have gone to a pottery fair. The potter Ōyama-san and his wife are friends of Hiroko's.

© Maekawa Tsukasa / *Dai-Tōkyō Binbō Seikatsu Manyuaru*, Kodansha

Hiroko: 大山さん、こんにちは。
Ōyama-san, konnichi wa.
"Ōyama-san, hello."

Ōyama: やあ、どーも、どーも。
Yā,　dōmo, dōmo.
"Well, well, hello."

- this *dōmo* might involve a touch of "Thank you for coming to the fair."

Hand to the head is a gesture of embarrassment. The college student who lives next to Kōsuke runs into Hiroko on the street. In the previous story, Kōsuke borrowed the student's bicycle (without permission) to take Hiroko to the station, but they encountered the student along the way. This mildly embarrassing situation is probably related to the hand-to-the-head gesture.

Hiroko: こんにちは。
Konnichi wa.
"Hi."

Student: あっ、ども。
A! Domo.
"Oh, hello."

© Maekawa Tsukasa / *Dai-Tōkyō Binbō Seikatsu Manyuaru*, Kodansha

If you're slightly flustered

Here are two variations on the hand-to-the-head gesture.

© Hijiri Hideo / *Naze ka Shōsuke*, Shogakukan

Secretary: 頑張ってね、笑介クン！
Ganbatte ne, Shōsuke-kun!
"Hang in there, Shōsuke!"
(PL2)

Shōsuke: ど、どーも。
Do, dōmo.
"Th-, thanks."

Shōsuke is faced with a difficult challenge here, and he's probably wondering how he will be able to pull this one off.

In this scene
Hikono and his charming co-worker, Asada-*kachō*, called on Kanetora-san, president of a taxi company. Kanetora-san is a rather outspoken individual.

© Torii Kazuyoshi / *Top wa Ore Da!!*, Shogakukan

Kanetora: いい　なあ、若いの…
Ii　nā, wakai no...
(it's) nice isn't it young one
"It's nice, isn't it, young man . . .

美人　　　　と一緒に　仕事　が　出来て。
Bijin　　　to issho ni shigoto ga　dekite.
beautiful woman together with work (subj.) can do
being able to work with a beautiful woman."
(PL2)

Hikono: あ、ドーモ。
A, dōmo.
"Ah, really."

A man of few words

In these two scenes from *Dai-Tōkyō Binbō Seikatsu Manyuaru*, Kōsuke shows his mastery of the art of the terse response.

Beautician:
お彼れさまでした。
O-tsukare-sama deshita.

- from the verb *tsukareru* = "become tired," this expression implies that the process of receiving a haircut was tiring, or that the customer was very patient. (This type of civility is usually not extended in English.)

Kōsuke:
ども。
Domo.

Daughter:
ごちそーさま。
Gochisō-sama.
"Thanks for the snack."

Carpenter:
ごっそさん。
Gosso-san.
(contracted, colloquial form of *gochisō-sama*)

Kōsuke:
ども。
Domo.

© Maekawa Tsukasa / *Dai-Tōkyō Binbō Seikatsu Manyuaru*, Kodansha

If you have a limited vocabulary

The only word this child can say is *dōmo*. The parakeet has a slightly larger vocabulary, but the first word it says to Kōsuke is *dōmo*. These examples are from two unrelated stories in *Dai-Tōkyō Binbō Seikatsu Manyuaru*.

© Maekawa Tsukasa / *Dai-Tōkyō Binbō Seikatsu Manyuaru*, Kodansha

© Maekawa Tsukasa / *Dai-Tōkyō Binbō Seikatsu Manyuaru*, Kodansha

Baby: ドーモ、ドーモ。
Dōmo, dōmo.

Parakeet: ドゥモ、ドゥモ。
Dōmo, dōmo.

- even in katakana there are different ways to write the long *ō*.

Good-bye

When leaving a house, office or shop you can use *dōmo* with the expression *o-jama shimashita*.

© Fujiko Fujio / *Mezame-sugita Otoko*, Shogakukan

Salesman: どうも、おじゃましました。
Dōmo, o-jama shimashita.
"Please pardon the intrusion." (PL3)

- *o-jama shimashita* literally means "I intruded/I was a nuisance." It's something like "Sorry to have bothered you" in English, but it's much more widely used.

© Kunitomo Yasuyuki / *Kikaku Ari*, Shogakukan

This *dōmo* could mean almost anything. In a sense it covers all the bases — no matter what had happened earlier between these two, *dōmo* is an appropriate response here.

A: そうか、じゃあここで。
Sō ka, jā koko de.
"I see, then (I'll say good-bye) here." (PL2)

B: どうも。
Dōmo.

Lesson 9 • *Dōzo*

Dōzo* is like *dōmo (see Lesson 8) in that it's added to expressions to make them more emphatic or polite, and, like *dōmo*, it can stand alone as a shortened form of those expressions. In many cases, the complete expressions would end in *–te kudasai*, meaning "please," but this is usually "please" in the sense of offering something or granting a favor, rather than making a request.

Offering a drink

One of the most common uses of *dōzo* is in offering food or drink to someone. In this scene, the drink has already been poured, and he is encouraging his guest to go ahead and partake.

Host: さあ どうぞ 飲んで ください。
Sā,   dōzo   nonde   kudasai.
"Well then, please have a drink/drink up." (PL3)

© Kobayashi Makoto / *What's Michael*, Kodansha

In this scene from *Dai-Tōkyō Binbō Seikatsu Manyuaru*, Kōsuke is approached by one member of a group of students who are drinking in a small restaurant.

© Maekawa Tsukasa / *Dai-Tōkyō Binbō Seikatsu Manyuaru*, Kodansha

Stranger: どーぞ。
Dōzo.
"Please [have a drink]." (PL3)

Sound FX: タン
Tan
(sound of the glass being put down on the counter)

• the dash after *do* makes it into a long *dō*. This is the way vowel sounds are normally elongated in katakana, but using this device with hiragana has something of a pop touch, like the spelling "nite" for "night" or "thru" for "through."

Offering more drinks

***Dōzo* can come before or after** the offer. Both of these examples use the word *o-hitotsu* — the honorific prefix *o-* added to *hitotsu*, the all-purpose "counter" meaning "one (object/thing)."

© Torii Kazuyoshi / *Top wa Ore Da!!*, Shogakukan

He wants to have a drink with the customer he is entertaining, but he's driving. The hand-to-the-head is a gesture of embarrassment or confusion.

<u>**Waitress:**</u> どうぞ、おひとつ。
Dōzo,   o-hitotsu.
please   (hon.)-one
"Please have one (a drink)." (PL3-4)

<u>**Customer:**</u> いえ、僕 は、その...
Ie,   boku wa, sono...
No   I   as-for that
"No, I, that is . . ." (PL indeterminate)

Michael has ventured into a cabaret, and appears to be in need of a drink at this point.

© Kobayashi Makoto / *What's Michael*, Kodansha

<u>**Hostess:**</u> さあ、おひとつ どうぞ。
Sā,   o-hitotsu   dōzo.
(colloq.) (hon.)-one   please
"Well, please have one (a drink)." (PL3-4)

<u>**Michael:**</u> む...
Mu...
"Mmm . . ."

Not just for alcoholic drinks

The tone of *dōzo* seems to be especially suited to offering an alcoholic beverage, but it's certainly not limited to such situations.

© Takahashi Rumiko / *Mezon Ikkoku*, Shogakukan

<u>**Girl:**</u> お茶をどおぞ。
Ocha o dōzo.
tea (obj.) please
"Please have some tea." (PL3-4)

<u>**Woman:**</u> あら、どうも。
Ara, dōmo.
"Oh, thanks." (PL3)

- the particle *o* after *ocha* implies a verb like *nonde kudasai* or the more formal/honorific *meshiagatte kudasai*.

The *dōzo* hand gesture

The tone or feeling of *dōzo* is expressed by this gesture with the open hand. The first scene is in a nightclub. The hostess is showing some customers to the table where their friends are already sitting (the kimono is an indication of an upscale establishment).

© Yamasaki & Kitami / *Tsuri-Baka Nisshi*, Shogakukan

Hostess: どうぞ、こちら です!!
Dōzo, kochira desu!!
please　this way　is
"Please, (it's) this way!!"
(PL3)

- *dōzo kochira e,* and *kochira (e) dōzo* are commonly used to show the way.

Please come in (and up)!

***Dōzo* is used** to invite people inside, although as shown in this example, there are two stages to coming "in" to a Japanese home.

Sound FX: ドキッ
Doki!

- here, he is putting the box down on the step leading (up) into the apartment.

Man: 掃除機　　お届け にまいりました。
Sōjiki o-todoke ni mairimashita.
vacuum cleaner delivery for　came
"I came to deliver the vacuum cleaner." (PL4)

Woman: どうぞ、中 へ 入って。
Dōzo, naka e haitte.
please　inside to　enter
"Please, come in(side) . . ." (PL2-3)

- *o-todoke* is the honorific/polite prefix *o-* added to *todoke,* from the verb *todokeru* = "deliver."
- *mairimashita* is a humble (PL4) verb, equivalent in this usage to *kimashita* = "came" (PL3).
- *naka* = "inside"
- *naka e haitte* is from *naka e hairu,* literally "come inside," but in a Japanese-style home this really means "step into the entranceway." This entranceway is on a lower level than the inside, so the verb *agaru* "come up/go up" is used to refer to actually entering the dwelling.

Just an aside to show the difference between *agaru* and *naka e hairu:*

Woman: いいから、上がってお茶 のんでいって よ。
Ii kara, agatte ocha nonde itte yo.
OK because come up-and tea drink-and go (emph.)
"It's all right, so come in and have some tea before you go." (PL2)

Man: じゃ、少し だけ...
Ja, sukoshi dake . . .
"Then, just a little." (PL indeterminate)

© Gyū & Kondō / *Eigyō Tenteko Nisshi*, Scholar

Please make yourself at home

One of the directors of this man's company has dropped in for an unexpected visit.

© Kobayashi Makoto / *What's Michael*, Kodansha

Host: さあ、どうぞ、どうぞ。
Sā, dōzo, dōzo.
"Well then, please, please."

ごゆっくり して って ください!!
Go-yukkuri shite tte kudasai!!
"Please relax and make yourself at home!!"
(PL3)

- in a preceding panel, the director announced that he stopped in because he was in the neighborhood. We used "Well then . . ." as a response to that, although *sā* might better be translated as "Well, well . . ."
- *yukkuri suru* = "take it slow/easy" → "make yourself at home." The honorific *go-* is added here.
- *shite tte* is a contraction of *shite itte* — *itte* is from the verb *iku* = "go," so this expression means "relax and make yourself at home (before you go)." This is similar to . . . *ocha nonde itte* in the last frame on the previous page.

The *kyaku-hiki*

Nightclubs and cabarets frequently have an employee who stands outside and lures in customers. This person is called a *kyaku-hiki* 客引き (*kyaku* = "customer," and *hiki* from the verb *hiku* = "pull in/attract").

© Kobayashi Makoto / *What's Michael*, Kodansha

The feline version,
from *What's Michael?*

Kyaku-hiki: どうぞ、いらっしゃいませー!!
Dōzo, irasshaimase–!!
"Please, come in (right this way)." (PL4)

© Tanaka Hiroshi / *Naku-na! Tanaka-kun*, Take Shobo

The human version,
from *Tanaka-kun.*

Sign: キャバレー
Kyabarē
Cabaret

Kyaku-hiki: どーぞー。
Dōzō.
"Please [come in]." (PL3)

"Sound" FX: ドキドキ
Doki doki
(Tanaka-kun's heart pounding)

Please, after you

She was next in line for a test ride, but she'd rather wait for a certain driver. This driver is obviously disappointed.

© Torii Kazuyoshi / *Top wa Ore Da!!*, Shogakukan

Young Lady: お先　　　にどうぞ。
O-saki　　ni　dōzo.
(hon.)-ahead　to　please
"Please, go ahead." (PL3)

Man: え...　いい　のかい?
E...　ii　no kai?
huh　OK　(explan.)?
"Huh . . . is it OK?" (PL2)

- *saki ni* = "before/ahead (of)." The *o-* prefix can only be described as "polite" since it's added no matter who goes first.
- *kai* = softer, friendlier version of *ka*, used mostly by males.

Go right ahead

Michael, the drug sniffing cat, has detected something in this man's bag. (It turns out to be catnip.)

© Kobayashi Makoto / *What's Michael*, Kodansha

Agent: ちょっと 中　を　確かめさせて もらいます　よ!!
Chotto　naka　o　tashikamesasete moraimasu　yo!!
a little　inside　(obj.)　will have you allow me to confirm　(emph.)
"I'll take the liberty of checking the contents!!" (PL2)

Passenger: はあ、どうぞ。
Hā, dōzo.
"Yes, please." (PL3)

- *tashikamesasete* is from the verb *tashikameru* = "confirm/check."

On the 2-way radio

In radio communications, *dōzo* is used like "over." This driver is not accustomed to using the radio.

Driver: ああ...聞こえるか?
Aa . . . kikoeru ka?
"Uh . . . can you hear me?" (PL2)

Dispatcher: ハイ　感度　　　良好　ですどうぞ。
Hai,　kando　ryōkō　desu. Dōzo.
yes sensitivity/reception good/favorable is　over
"Yes, loud and clear. Over." (PL3)

© Gyū & Kondō / *Eigyō Tenteko Nisshi*, Scholar

Driver: あと　二台、　メーカー に
Ato　ni-dai　mēkā　ni
more　2 (-count)　maker　from

暖房器　TON-30 の　発注　を 願います。どうぞ。
danbōki TON-sanjū no hatchū　o　negaimasu. Dōzo.
heater(s)　model #　's ordering (obj.)　I request　over
"Please order two more TON-30 heaters from the manufacturer. Over." (PL3)

More in the nature of a request

In these last three examples, *dōzo* is used to make requests. First, an ATM "money machine" uses *dōzo* to ask/invite customers to enter their secret code number.

<u>ATM screen:</u> 暗証　　番号　を　どうぞ。
Anshō bangō o dōzo.
secret code number (obj.) please
"Your secret number, please."

<u>Woman:</u> えーっと、私の　たんじょう日...
Ee tto, watashi no tanjōbi...
(pause) my birthday
"Uuh, my birthday (is) . . ."

- this wording is not universal. Some machines say *Anshō bangō o oshite kudasai* ("Please enter/push your secret number").

© Usui Yoshihito / *Kureyon Shinchan*, Futabasha

If you would . . .

This doctor is addressing a group and asks/invites them to think about what would happen "if (they developed a serious illness)."

© Hanai & Miyahara / *Tottemo I-in*, Shogakukan

<u>Doctor:</u> どうぞ皆さん、
Dōzo mina-san,
please everyone-hon.

"もし" と いうこと を 考えて下さい。
"moshi" to iu koto o kangaete kudasai.
if quote say thing (obj.) please think about
"Please, everyone, think about what might happen (think about 'if')." (PL3)

Kudasai vs. *Dōzo*

This *dōzo* is obviously in the nature of an invitation, while this *kudasai* is used in a (desperate) request. Hikono-san is entertaining a potential customer who turned out to have quite a healthy appetite.

<u>Sound FX:</u> シー
Shii
(sucking in air as he picks his teeth)

<u>Counterman:</u> またどうぞー。
Mata dōzo–.
"Please (come) again." (PL3)

<u>Hikono:</u> 領収書下さい。
Ryōshūsho kudasai.
"Please give me a receipt." (PL3)

© Torii Kazuyoshi / *Top wa Ore Da!!*, Shogakukan

Lesson 10 • *Baka,* the Basic Insult

In the Japanese-English dictionary, *baka* is listed as "fool," or "idiot." This sounds pretty mild to the Western ear, and while *baka* is indeed used in this mild, literal sense, with the proper forcefulness of delivery, *baka* can have as much impact as words which are considered "profane" in English. This range of uses makes *baka* one of the most widely used "insults" in the Japanese language. Even if you don't plan to insult anyone, an understanding of the concept of "*baka*" is necessary for a complete understanding of Japanese.

Horse + deer = fool?

Baka can be written with the kanji for "horse" (馬) and "deer" (鹿). This is an example of *ateji*, or kanji which are used for their sound/reading, rather than their inherent meaning. It's not surprising that a child would not be able to read this word, and in the example below, the child has asked his mother, who is explaining the word *baka* to him.

© Tanaka Makoto /
Gyanburu Rēsā, Kodansha

Mother: えー と ね、 この 字 は 馬 って
Ē to ne, kono ji wa uma tte
uuh (quote) (colloq.) this character as-for horse (quote)

読む の。 こっち は 鹿 ね
yomu no. Kotchi wa shika ne.
read (explan.) this as-for deer (colloq.)
"Uuh, you read this character 'horse.' This one is 'deer.'" (PL2)

馬 と 鹿 で バカ って 読む の よ!
Uma to shika de baka tte yomu no yo!
horse and deer with baka (quote) read (explan.) (emph.)
"'Horse' and 'deer' together are read 'baka!'" (PL2)

- *tte* is used like the quotative particle *to* here.
- *kotchi* is a colloquial form of *kochira.*

Why is *baka* written with these kanji? We were not able to come up with a definitive explanation, but here is a little background:

- Other kanji have been used to write *baka*, but now 馬鹿 is pretty much the standard. Katakana is also frequently used to write *baka* in manga, especially when the delivery is forceful.
- There is a story in Chinese history of a leader who called a stag a horse to test his subjects — he wanted to see if they would be "yes men" or if they would stand up to him. It may be that the Japanese person who assigned these kanji to *baka* knew of that story.
- It could be these kanji were chosen simply because horses and deer are "dumb" animals. *Ba* is the standard reading for *uma* in combinations, so this was an easy choice, but *shika* is generally read *roku* when combined with another kanji, so it appears that the assigner of *ateji* was making a force fit for the second kanji.

Baka = "fool"

Realizing he has been tricked (by a scheming businesswoman), this young man smashes the model of his new building to the floor.

© Gen Tarō / *Yume no Hishō,* Shogakukan

Muramatsu: バカ　だ!!
Baka   da!!
fool/idiot am
"(I'm) a fool!!" (PL2)

俺　は　大バカ　だ　よーっ!!
Ore wa ōbaka da yō!!
I/me as-for big fool am (emph.)
"I'm a big fool!!" (PL2)

- *ore* is an abrupt, masculine word for "I/me."

Baka, the expletive

The letter is from her boyfriend who has left town, but didn't tell her beforehand because it would make it harder to say good-bye. In a way, she's calling him a fool, but this use of *baka* is more like a one-word expletive. The kanji are used here, but as shown in the following examples, *baka* is more frequently written in katakana.

Girl: 馬鹿！
Baka!
"Fool!"

FX: ビリッ！
Biri!
(sound of ripping up letter)

© Funazaki & Miyama / *Uwasa no Tamasaburō,* Shogakukan

"This fool" = "You fool"

This scene is from the series 釣りバカ日誌 *Tsuri-Baka Nisshi* ("Diary of a Fishing Nut"). The term *tsuri-baka* really refers to someone who is "crazy" about fishing, but this particular character (shown here taking a thrashing from his boss), seems to be *baka* in the general sense of the word as well. *Kono baka* literally means "This fool/idiot," but it's used when addressing the party in question, like "You fool/idiot" would be in English.

© Yamasaki & Kitami / *Tsuri-Baka Nisshi,* Shogakukan

Boss: 聞いてん のか、この バカッ？
Kiiten no ka, kono baka!?
listening ? this fool
"Are you listening (to me), you idiot?" (PL2-1)

- *kiiten (no ka)* is a contraction of *kiite-iru (no ka)*.
- the small *tsu* (ツ) at the end of the sentence indicates it is cut off sharply. We use an exclamation mark to reflect this style of delivery.

© Yajima & Hirokane / *Ningen Kōsaten*, Shogakukan

Combinations: *baka* + *mono*

The suffix –*mono*, meaning "person" is frequently added to *baka*. This high school boy was bullying a smaller child, but when the bully taunts the child about his mother working in a cabaret, the old man loses his temper.

Old Man: 馬鹿者。
Bakamono.
"You idiot!" → **"You little jerk!"**

Sound FX: ヴァシィッ
Vashii!
(the "whack" of a slender cane)

Boy: うわッ。
Uwa!
(exclamation)

© Ōtani & Sadayasu / *Shishi no Gotoku*, Kodansha

The suffix –*mono* can be shortened to –*mon*, as in this example.

Hirano: バカモン。
Bakamon.
"You SOB."

FX: がきっ
Gaki!
(effect of grabbing hold of his opponent)

baka + *yarō*

© Wakabayashi Kenji / *Heisei Arashiyama Ikka*, Shogakukan

Strictly speaking, *yarō* ("guy/fellow") refers to a male. *Yarō* can also be used as an insult, and depending on the tone of voice, *kono yarō* can be something like "you SOB!" When used as an insult, the gender distinction becomes less critical. In this scene, the father is yelling at his entire family (wife, daughter, and son) for bringing along too much unnecessary equipment on a camping trip (he winds up carrying it).

Father: ばかやろー!!
Bakayarō!!
"Idiot(s)!!"

baka + noun

This cat has a reputation as a connoisseur of fine food, but it used this man's specially prepared seafood dish as kitty litter. If the cat were a human being, he might be calling it *bakayarō*, but *baka* can also be combined with more specific nouns. Other examples are: *baka-musuko* ("idiot son"), *baka-shōjiki* ("honesty to the point of being stupid/too much honesty for one's own good").

© Tomisawa Chinatsu / *Katsushika Kyū*, Shogakukan

Kyū-san: この　バカ猫　がー!!
Kono baka-neko ga–!!
this　idiot cat　(subj.)
"You stupid #@*% cat!!" (PL1)

Cat: フギャーフギャー
Fugyā　fugyā
(yowling sound)

- *baka-neko* could be translated simply as "fool cat," but given the intensity of this man's expression, he would probably be using a "cussword" in English.
- the particle *ga* is frequently added on, implying a complete thought. It also serves to emphasize the subject of that thought (*baka-neko*).

baka as an adjective

The ending *-na* is added to certain nouns to make adjectives, and *baka-na* means "foolish/crazy/stupid." This man's old childhood enemy has died as a vagrant and is about to be cremated as a "John Doe."

© Yajima & Hirokane / *Ningen Kōsaten,* Shogakukan

そんな　馬鹿な　こと　は　　ないだろう!!
Sonna　baka-na　koto　wa　　nai darō!!
such a　crazy　thing　as-for　does not exist/can't be
"That's crazy!" (PL2)

死んでいる　と　　は　　いえ、　　人間　に対して...
Shinde-iru　to　　wa　　ie,　　ningen ni taishite...
is dead　(quote)　as-for　can be said　human being　to/toward
"Even though (he's) dead, (they can't do such a thing) to a human being . . ."
→ **"Even if he's dead, he's still a human being . . ."**

© Nabeshima & Maekawa / *Hyōden no Torakutā,* Shogakukan

This man has just heard some shocking news about a police raid on a company dormitory. It's as if he is too shocked to come out with a complete sentence—all he can manage is the first few words.

そ、そんな　バカな!!
So, sonna　baka-na!!
"Su, such a crazy . . .!!"
→ **"That's crazy!"** or **"That can't be!!"** (PL2)

- this can be shortened even more to simply *Sonna . . .*
- another variation is *Baka-na . . .* (by itself)

Expressions using *baka*

Baka **is used** in a number of common expressions, such as *baka (o) iu*, literally "talk foolishness." In this case, *baka* means "foolishness/nonsense," rather than "fool."

© Yamasaki & Kitami / *Tsuri-Baka Nisshi*, Shogakukan

President: バカ 言っちゃ いかん!!
Baka itcha ikan!!
foolishness if say/talk won't do
"Don't talk foolishness!!"
(PL2)

- *itcha* is a contraction of *itte wa*, from *iu* ("say").
- *ikan* is used like *ikenai* ("must not/should not"), used primarily by older males.

In this scene, from *Tsuri-Baka Nisshi*, Hamazaki (with the big grin) has just complimented Takejō on his English ability. Given Hamazaki's facetious nature, Takejō has reason to suspect he is being made fun of.

© Yamasaki & Kitami / *Tsuri-Baka Nisshi*, Shogakukan

Takejō: バカ に してる ん です か!!
Baka ni shite-ru n desu ka!!
fool into making (explan.) are (you) ?
"Are you making fun of me?!" (PL3)

Somewhat milder than *baka*

© Kunitomo Yasuyuki / *Kikaku Ari*, Shogakukan

This middle-aged businessman has just been told by his teenage daughter that working too hard was a crime (*hanzai*).

Father: ばかばかしい!
Baka-bakashii!
"Ridiculous!" (PL2)

なに が 犯罪 だ!!
Nani ga hanzai da!!
what (subj.) crime is
"What's the crime (about working too much)!!" (PL2)

Sound FX: ずずー
Zu zū
(slurping sound of drinking soup)

Baka in proverbs & folk sayings

Tsuyoshi has been challenged to jump off the roof of the house in order to prove his determination in a dispute about his sister's marriage.

© Nagamatsu Kiyoshi / *Tsuyoshi, Shikkari Shinasai*, Kodansha

Sister: ツヨシ なら やる わね。
Tsuyoshi nara yaru wa ne.
(name) if will do (it) (fem. colloq.)
"Tsuyoshi is just the kind of person who would do it (jump off the roof)." (PL2)

Mother: そう。 バカ と 煙 は
Sō. Baka to kemuri wa
right fool and smoke as-for

高い 所 が 得意な の よ。
takai tokoro ga tokui na no yo.
high places (subj.) are specialty (explan.) (emph.)
"That's right. Smoke and fools both specialize in/ are good at high places." (PL2-Fem.)

• this is a slight variation on the saying: *Baka to kemuri wa takai tokoro ga suki.* ("Fools and smoke like high places") or . . . *takai tokoro ni noboru* (". . . rise to high places").

From the series *Urusei Yatsura*, Cherry, the deranged monk, reacts to the news that Ataru has caught cold.

© Takahashi Rumiko / *Urusei Yatsura*, Shogakukan

Cherry: バカ は カゼ を ひかん
Baka wa kaze o hikan
fool as-for cold (obj.) doesn't catch

と いう が のう...
to iu ga nō...
(quote) say but (colloq.)
"They say that a fool doesn't catch colds, but . . ." (PL2)

Pāma: 今年 の カゼ は
Kotoshi no kaze wa
this year 's cold(s) as-for

バカ でも ひく そう だ!
baka de mo hiku sō da!
fool even catch (hearsay) is
"I hear that even fools catch this year's colds!" (PL2)

• *hikan* is a masculine form of *hikanai*, the plain/ abrupt past of *hiku* ("catch [a cold]").
• using *nō* at the end of a sentence like *nā* or *nē* is typical of the speech of older people.
• . . . *sō da* is used to report what you heard.

Lesson 11 • *Shitsurei* 失礼

Shitsurei is written with two kanji meaning "lose" (失 *shitsu*) and "polite-ness/manners" (礼 *rei*). The word *shitsurei* is a noun meaning "rudeness" or "bad manners," but students usually encounter it first in the expression *shitsurei shimashita*, literally "I have committed a rudeness," → "I'm sorry/Excuse me." The non-past form, *shitsurei shimasu*, literally "I (will) commit a rudeness," is typically used to apologize in advance for anything that might be considered a disturbance, interruption, or impropriety. Like "Excuse me," *shitsurei shimasu* is also used in ways that are fairly idiomatic — for example, as a kind of "good-bye." To illustrate these and other uses, we'll let the manga do the talking.

Shitsurei as an apology

This man is late for a luncheon of business leaders. He apologizes as he enters the room. In this case, he could have used *sumimasen* instead of *shiturei shimashita* → *Osoku natte sumimasen*.

遅くなって　失礼しました。
Osoku natte   shitsurei shimashita.
became late-and   (I) was impolite
"Excuse me for being late." (PL3)

- *osoku* is the adverb form of *osoi* ("late").
- *natte* is from the verb *naru* ("become"). The *-te* form functions here to express a cause–effect situation ("I am late and [as a result] I have committed a rudeness.")

© Yamasaki & Kitami / *Tsuri-Baka Nisshi,* Shogakukan

This salaryman apologizes after being reprimanded by one of his female co-workers. His response can be considered an abbreviated form of *shitsurei shimashita.*

© Gyū & Kondō / *Eigyō Tenteko Nisshi,* Scholar

OL: トイレ出たら　手　を　洗って下さい!!
Toire detara   te   o aratte kudasai!!
toilet　when leave　hands　(obj.)　please wash
"When you come out of the toilet, please wash your hands!!" (PL3)

Salaryman: あ ... 失礼。
A ... Shitsurei.
"Oh ... sorry."

- *toire* is a katakana version of "toilet." Strictly speaking, the particle *o* should follow *toire*.
- *detara* is a conditional form of the verb *deru* ("leave/go out/come out").
- *te* = hands
- *aratte* is from the verb *arau* ("wash").

Three cases for *shitsurei*

Making a cold call on a taxi company, this young car salesman introduces himself, and then immediately sits down and pulls out a brochure about his company's line of automobiles. Jumping right into the sales pitch without establishing rapport with the prospect and sitting down without being asked would be considered impolite in almost any culture. He makes a cursory apology as he makes himself at home and whips out the sales material.

Salesman: ちょっと 失礼 します。
Chotto shitsurei shimasu.
"Excuse me (just a little)." (PL3)

- *chotto* = "a little"

© Torii Kazuyoshi / *Top wa Ore Da!!*, Shogakukan

He is scolded by the prospect for not doing his "homework" on their business and not being better prepared — prepared to give a big discount, that is. The prospect holds out the carrot of a big sale, but insists on talking with someone higher up who is ready to deal. Here, the salesman is running out the door, apparently to get his boss to come back with him and close the sale. Although *Shitsurei shimashita* can be used in an idiomatic way when departing, in this case it has the nature of a real apology.

Salesman: 失礼 しましたあー!!
Shitsurei shimashitā!!
"Excuse me!!" (PL3)

© Torii Kazuyoshi / *Top wa Ore Da!!*, Shogakukan

Even if your manners were impeccable, it's considered good form to apologize for your behavior during your previous encounter. In this case, the young salesman really has something to apologize for. The prospect is surprised, and slightly impressed, that the salesman had the gumption to come back.

© Torii Kazuyoshi / *Top wa Ore Da!!*, Shogakukan

Prospect: ほー、 よく 来た なあ。
Hō, yoku kita nā.
(exclam.) well/persistently came (colloq.)
"Heh, I'm surprised to see you." (PL2)

Salesman: 昨日 は どうも 失礼しました。
Sakujitsu wa dōmo shitsurei shimashita.
yesterday as-for indeed I was impolite
An American might say something like **"Thanks for your time yesterday,"** but this salesman is literally saying **"I was very impolite yesterday."** (PL3)

- *yoku* is the adverb form of *yoi* ("good"), and *kita* is the plain/abrupt past form of *kuru* ("come"). Followed by a verb, *yoku* can give the feeling that the speaker is impressed/surprised
- *sakujitsu* is a more formal equivalent of *kinō* ("yesterday").

Shitsurei when entering

It's good manners to say *shitsurei shimasu* when entering someone else's room or office, especially if the person is of higher status than you. The feeling is that you are apologizing for intruding on their space. Here the maid brings tea to a guest at an inn.

> **Maid:** 失礼　します。
> *Shitsurei shimasu.*
> **"Excuse me."** (PL3)
>
> **Sound FX:** スーッ
> *Sū!*
> (sound/effect of door sliding open)

© Yamamoto Mitsuhiko / Dosa-resurā Densetsu 6, Scholar

In the scene below, a camera crew has arrived to photograph this couple's dancing cat (named Michael). Even though they are being welcomed in, the young lady gives a polite *shitsurei shimasu* before she actually enters their home.

© Kobayashi Makoto / *What's Michael*, Kodansha

> **Husband:** どうも、お待ちしておりました。
> *Dōmo,　omachi shite-orimashita.*
> **"We've been waiting (for you)."** (PL4)
>
> **Wife:** さあ、どうぞ、どうぞ。
> *Sā,　dōzo,　dōzo.*
> **"Well, please, please (come in)."** (PL3)
>
> **Reporter:** それ じゃ 失礼　しまーす。
> *Sore　ja shitsurei shima–su.*
> **"Then, excuse me."** (PL3)

Rough but friendly: this man's friend is depressed and sulking alone in his car. He's getting into the car to cheer up his friend, and he uses the word *shitsurei* as a token apology for his "intrusion," but the informal *suru* (PL2), and the rough emphatic ending *zo* show that this use of *shitsurei* is rather idiomatic.

> **Friend:** 失礼　するぞ。
> *Shitsurei suru zo.*
> **"Hey, I'm gettin' in!"** (PL2)
>
> **Sound FX:** ガチャッ
> *Gacha!*
> (sound of car door opening)

© Yajima & Hirokane / *Ningen Kōsaten*, Shogakukan

Shitsurei when leaving

It's already past "quitting time," but since some of her co-workers are still in the office, she is apologizing for leaving ahead of them. The expression *o-saki ni* literally means "ahead of/in front of," and it can be used alone as a shortened form of this "Goodbye."

© Gyū & Kondō / *Eigyō Tenteko Nisshi,* Scholar

Secretary: お先 に 失礼します。
O-saki ni shitsurei shimasu.
"Goodbye." (PL3)

Chief: お疲れさま。
Otsukare-sama.
"Goodbye." (PL3)

- *otsukare-sama* is another expression that can be used as a "Goodbye." It comes from the verb *tsukareru* ("become tired"), and is essentially a way of thanking someone for his/her hard work, so it can also be used at the end of any job or significant exertion, even when no one is ready to leave yet.

After a meeting, this businessman uses the expression *shitsurei shimasu* somewhat like "Excuse myself" in English — to indicate that he's leaving.

© Tamiya & Shinohara / *Boss,* Shogakukan

Businessman: それじゃ、 私 は このへんで
Sore ja, watashi wa kono hen de
then/in that case I/me as-for about now

失礼します よ!!
shitsurei shimasu yo!!
will be impolite (emph.)
"Well then, I'll excuse myself at this point." (PL3)

- *hen,* which can refer to a geographical "area/neighborhood," in this case refers to a place in time, so *kono hen* = "about now/about this time."

She is excusing herself temporarily from the table at a restaurant, so she adds *sukoshi* ("a little") to the beginning of the phrase. The man obscured by her "balloon" in this frame has asked to talk to her, and her boss is wondering what it's about.

© Tsukamoto Tomoko / *Karā-na Ai,* Shogakukan

Woman: ごめんなさい、専務、 少し 失礼します。
Gomen-nasai, senmu, sukoshi shitsurei shimasu.
pardon (me) (title) a little (I) will be impolite
"I'm sorry sir, excuse me just a moment." (PL3)

Sound FX: ガタッ
Gata!
(sound of chair being pushed back)

Senmu: えっ
E!
(thinking) **"Huh?"**

- *senmu* = "managing director," that is, she's calling him by his title (as employees usually do). In English, she would probably be calling him Mr. (family name). We don't know his name, so we used "sir," although this doesn't really convey the tone of *senmu.*

You are being *shitsurei*

In the examples so far, *shitsurei* has been used as an apology for one's own behavior. In the following examples, it's used to refer to someone else's behavior.

In the first scene, *shitsurei* is used in its basic form, as a noun. The husband has been expressing his critical views of the entire medical profession in front of a doctor who is offering him a new treatment for his ailment. His wife finally tries to restrain him.

Wife: あなた、言いすぎ　よ。　失礼　だ　わ!
Anata,   iisugi   yo.   Shitsurei da wa!
you   saying too much (emph.) rudeness is (fem.)
"Honey, you're going too far (saying too much). It's rude!" (PL2-Fem.)

Husband: うるさいッ!!
Urusai!!
noisy/bothersome
"Shut up!!" (PL1)

- *anata* ("you") is used like "honey/dear" by Japanese wives when speaking to their husbands.
- *iisugi* = "saying too much" → "expressing extreme views."

© Hanai & Miyahara / *Tottemo I'in,* Shogakukan

The *oyaji*-gal has none of the gentle, obedient nature of the traditional Japanese woman. In this rather exaggerated example, Ms. Arashiyama pushes aside her immediate supervisor to complain directly to the department head about the treatment of one of her co-workers.

Supervisor: 嵐山くん、　　　キミ ちょっと 失礼　だ　よ。
Arashiyama-kun, kimi   chotto shitsurei da   yo.
(name)   you a little rudeness is/are (emph.)
さがりたまえ!!
Sagaritamae!!
withdraw/step back
"Arashiyama, you're being a little rude! Step back!!" (PL2)

Sound FX: ガン
Gan
Bang

Supervisor: あ...
A...
"Ah..."

© Wakabayashi Kenji / *Arashiyama Ikka,* Shogakukan

The adjective form

This woman is reacting to a snide remark that her boyfriend is an upstart who has nothing but his money to recommend him. The ending *-na* can be added to some nouns such as *shitsurei* to make an adjective form. Her exclamation implies a complete thought like *Shitsurei-na koto* ("[What a] rude thing [to say].”), or *Shitsurei-na hito* ("[What a] rude person!”).

失礼な!
Shitsurei-na!
"How rude!" (PL2)

© Kariya & Hanasaki / *Oishinbo,* Shogakukan

"Excuse me, but . . ."

The hotel has received a complaint about noise being made by other members of this woman's party. Before mentioning the problem, this hotel employee confirms that she is affiliated with the offending group — Tokyo World (an automobile sales company).

Hotel Employee: あのう、失礼 です が ...
Anō,   shitsurei desu ga,
(pause) impolite is/are but

東京ワールド の 方 です か?
Tōkyō Wārudo no kata desu ka?
(company name) of person is/are ?
"Uhh, excuse me, but are you with Tokyo World?" (PL3)

Sound FX: カチャ
Kacha
Click (sound of lock turning over)

• *kata* ("person") is one step politer than *hito*.

© Torii Kazuyoshi / *Top wa Ore Da!!*, Shogakukan

On the phone

It sounds like a wrong number, but actually she's faking it. She was talking to her boyfriend when her boss walked into the room.

© Miyama Noboru / *Rat*, Shogakukan

Secretary: 失礼 です が どなた に おかけ です か?
Shitsurei desu ga, donata ni o-kake desu ka?
impolite is but who to calling are ?
"Excuse me, but who are you calling?" (PL3)

• *donata* ("who") is more polite/formal than *dare*.
• *o-kake* is from the verb *kakeru* ("call [on the phone]"). This is a polite/honorific form.

It's hard to say goodbye without sounding abrupt, so *shitsurei shimasu* is a favorite way to end phone conversations.

© Tsukamoto Tomoko / *Karā-na Ai*, Shogakukan

Exec: では そーゆー こと で。
De wa, sō yū   koto   de.
then that kind of thing/arrangement with
"Then that'll be our arrangement,"

はい、では 失礼しますっ。
hai, de wa shitsurei shimasu!!
yes then I will be impolite
"Right, then, excuse me (goodbye)." (PL3)

Sound FX: ガチャン
Gachan
(sound of hanging up the phone)

• the double, small *tsu* at the end of *shimasu* indicate that it's cut off sharply — just like this lesson!

Lesson 12 • *Ii* — the "Good" Word

***Ii* basically means** "good," or "nice," but in idiomatic usage it takes on a wide range of meanings — something like "All right" or "OK" in English. Some of the examples in this lesson are fairly straightforward, but we also look at one group of common uses that can cause confusion for non-native (as well as native!) speakers. The confusion generally results from the fact that a simple *ii desu* can mean "(That would be) nice" → "Yes," or, "(That's) all right" → "No, thank you." Context, facial expression, and tone of voice usually make the intended meaning clear, but sometimes it's necessary to make a verbal clarification/elaboration. In many cases there are alternative expressions, such as *o-negai shimasu*, or *arigatō gozaimasu* which are safer, although they don't have the succinct Japanese charm of a simple *ii desu*.

There is no single, simple rule that will prevent all misunderstandings, and as is frequently the case, getting a "feel" for this word is perhaps the best approach.

The most basic usage

As a simple adjective meaning "good/nice," *ii* can come before the word it modifies, as in this example.

© Matsumoto Daiyō / *Zero,* Shogakukan

いい 天気 っす ね。
Ii   tenki   ssu   ne.
"Nice weather, isn't it." (PL3-2)

- the *ssu* after *tenki* is a contraction of *desu*. He is speaking to a slightly older, more experienced athlete, and is showing respect in an informal way.

Ii when saying "Yes"

In these examples, *ii* is used to mean "Yes."

A: クルマ　貸してくれない　か　な?
Kuruma　kashite kurenai　ka　na?
car　wouldn't do favor of lending　?　(colloq.)
"I wonder if you'd lend me your car?" (PL2)

B: あー いいよ。
Ā,　ii yo.
"Oh, sure." (PL2)

- *kashite* is from the verb *kasu* ("lend").
- *kurenai* is the plain/abrupt negative of *kureru* = "give/do for me/us," used among peers or to subordinates.
- his response is like a contraction of *Kashite mo ii* ("It would be all right to lend . . .").

© Tanaka Hiroshi / *Naku-na! Tanaka-kun,* Take Shobo

He's remembering how she accepted when he asked her out. Perhaps he said something like *O-cha de mo nomi ni ikanai?*

Arrow: 初　デート
Hatsu dēto
First date

Her: お茶 のむ ぐらい なら いい　わ。
Ocha nomu　gurai　nara　ii　wa.
tea　drink　only/just　if　good/OK　(fem. colloq.)
"If it's just for tea, then OK." (PL2-fem.)

- *gurai* or *kurai* means "about/to the extent of," so *Ocha nomu gurai* means "to the extent of drinking tea" → "just drinking tea."
- her use of *ii* could be construed as a contraction of *Itte mo ii* ("It would be all right to go").

© Shōji Sadao / *Sararii-man Senka,* Kodansha

Ii when saying "No"

It's pretty clear that he's saying "No, that's all right," but if he had elongated the *iya* (to *iyā*) and added a *ne* after *ii* (*ii ne*), and if he were smiling, he could be saying "That would be nice."

Wife: あなた、お食事 は?
Anata,　o-shokuji　wa?
you　meal/food as-for
"Dear, (how about) your dinner?" (PL unclear)

Husband: いや、いい。
Iya,　ii.
"No, (that's) all right." (PL2)

- Japanese wives typically call their husbands *anata* (literally "you"). We translated it as "Dear," but *anata* could be considered less openly affectionate (although this also depends on the tone of voice).
- adding the polite/honorific prefix *o-* to *shokuji* ("meal/food") has something of a feminine touch in this informal situation, but it's not strange for a man to say *o-shokuji* in a formal situation, or when referring to a superior's meal/food.

© Kawaguchi Kaiji / *Medusa,* Shogakukan

They all elaborate

In all examples on this and the facing page, the speaker elaborates in order to clarify exactly what is meant by *ii*.

Visiting his in-laws, this young man clarifies his response by specifying *boku* (masculine word for "I/me") as the subject of *ii* — *Boku (wa) ii desu yo* means "I am (doing) fine/all right" → "No thank you." The *yo* at the end is simply for emphasis.

© Nishi & Hashimoto / *Fūfu Seikatsu*, Shogakukan

<u>**Father:**</u> うん、 これ は 潔クン が 食べなさい。
Un, kore wa Kiyoshi-kun ga tabenasai.
Uhm this as-for (name-hon.) (subj.) eat
"Uhm, you have this, Kiyoshi." (PL3)

<u>**Kiyoshi:**</u> え... 僕 いい です よ。お義父さん が...
E... boku, ii desu yo. Otōsan ga...
huh I/me OK am (emph.) father (subj.)
"Huh . . . I'm doing fine, Father (you have it)." (PL3)

- the reading *Otōsan* ("father") is shown beside kanji which would normally be read *gifu* ("father-in-law"). Calling one's in-laws "Father" and "Mother" is standard practice, but the kanji is used to show the actual relationship.

From the series *Aji-Ichimonme*, Ihashi-san is visiting the home of a young co-worker, and his newlywed wife. They are living in a small, one-room apartment, and the sweat popping off Ihashi's face in the second frame probably indicates slight embarrassment at the idea of spending the night in the same room with newlyweds. He elaborates by specifying what action he is going to (or is willing to) take.

<u>**Wife:**</u> 誠ちゃん、 今夜 伊橋さん に 泊って頂いたら?
Mako-chan, Kon'ya Ihashi-san ni tomatte itadaitara?
(name) tonight (name) by have spend the night
"Why don't we have Ihashi-san stay with us tonight?"

<u>**Ihashi:**</u> い...いい です よ、
I... ii desu yo,
OK is (emph.)

帰ります から。
kaerimasu kara.
will go home because
"Th-that's all right, (because) I'll go home/I'm going home." (PL3)

- Ihashi-san instinctively uses "inverted syntax" The standard word order for his sentence would be *Kaerimasu kara, ii desu yo.* "I'm going/I'll go home, so that's all right."

© Abe & Kurata / *Aji Ichimonme*, Shogakukan

She fixed spaghetti for dinner three days in a row. He is a temperamental artist, and the incident apparently upset him so much that he lost his appetite.

© Akehi Masao / *Furuete Nemure,* Shueisha

Woman: 怒らないで... 何か　他のもの　作る　から。
Okoranaide . . . Nani ka hoka no mono tsukuru kara.
not get mad　　something　other thing　will make　because
"Don't get mad . . . (because) I'll make something else."
(PL2)

Artist: いい　よ。　　もう　　いらない!
Ii　yo.　　mō　　iranai!
OK　(emph.)　more/anymore　don't need
"That's all right. I'm not hungry anymore!" (PL2)

- *okoranaide* is from the verb *okoru* ("become angry"). It's an abbreviation of *okoranaide kudasai* ("Please don't get mad").
- *hoka no mono* = "a different thing/something else"

She declines his invitation to watch while he feeds his Venus' flytraps. In this story, the mother is concerned because her son is 32 and still single. Part of the problem is his hobby.

© Saigan Ryōhei / *San-Chōme no Yūhi,* Shogakukan

Son: 母さん　も　ちょっと　来て見てごらん　よ。
Kāsan mo chotto kite mite goran yo.
mother　also　a little　come-and-see　(emph.)
"Mom, you come watch a little too."

ハエジゴク　に　ハエ　を　食べさせてる　んだ。
Hae-jigoku ni hae o tabesasete-ru n da.
Venus flytrap　to　flies　(obj.)　am feeding　(explan.)-am

おもしろい　よ。
omoshiroi　yo.
interesting　(emph.)
"I'm feeding flies to (my) Venus' flytraps. It's fun." (PL2)

Mother: いい　わよ、　気色悪い。
Ii　wa yo, kishoku warui.
OK　(fem. emph.)　disgusting
"That's all right, it's disgusting." (PL2)

- *hae* 蝿 = "fly," and *jigoku* 地獄 = "hell," so a Venus' flytrap is called a "Fly Hell" in colloquial Japanese. The biological Japanese name is *haetori-gusa* 蝿取草.

Doubled for emphasis . . .

No elaboration is made in the next two examples. In this first scene, the angry young man goes back to confront the driver of the car that bumped into his.

オイッ
Oi!
"Hey!" (PL1)

いいです、いいです。
Ii desu,   ii desu.
"That's all right, that's all right."
(PL3)

© Shōji Sadao / *Sararii-man Senka*, Kodansha

His plan is to leave the old date on the camera so it will look like they were eating watermelon in April (a luxury).

Wife: いま 61年 の 7月 よ
Ima rokujūichi-nen no shichi-gatsu yo.
now   61st year   's   July   (emph.)
"It's (now) July of '86, you know."
(PL2)

Husband: いいの、いいの。
Ii no,   ii no.
"It's OK, it's OK." (PL2)

• the year 61 is Shōwa 61 = 1986.

© Shōji Sadao / *Sararii-man Senka*, Kodansha

In propositions

One of the more frequently used lines in making a proposition is *Ii darō*, or its close cousin *Ii ja nai (ka)* which might look like "Isn't it/Wouldn't it be good," but actually means, "Isn't it/wouldn't it be all right?" It's vague enough that either party can claim verbal misunderstanding if the answer is "No." In this example, she knows exactly what he's talking about.

Man: 今日 こそ いい だろう?
Kyō koso ii darō?
today for sure OK isn't it
"Today for sure, it's OK, isn't it?" (PL2)

なあ。
Nā.
"Isn't it."

Woman: 何 が さ?
Nani ga sa?
what (subj.) (colloq.)
"What is (OK)?" (PL2)

© Akiyama Jōji / *Haguregumo*, Shogakukan

• in this case *sa* is used as an emphatic ending, but it's arguably less of a definite "No" than *Nani ga yo*!

In response to "Thank you"

This is an example of *Sumimasen* being used like "Thank you." She is a friend, helping this down-on-his-luck pro golfer get ready for a tournament. This *Sumimasen* could carry a touch of apology — "I apologize for causing you to go to so much trouble on my behalf."

© Takeda & Takai / *Oribe Kinjirō,* Shogakukan

<u>Golfer:</u> すみません。
Sumimasen.
"I appreciate it."
(PL3)

<u>Friend:</u> いいのよ。
Ii no yo.
"That's all right."
(PL2)

A little rough — *Ii ya*

The man he wants to see is on leave, and he doesn't want to talk to the one filling in.

© Hayashi & Takai / *Yamaguchi Roppeita,* Shogakukan

<u>Man:</u> なんだ... じゃ、 いい や。
Nan da... ja, ii ya.
what is it? then/in that case OK (colloq.)
"Oh well . . . then, forget it." (PL2)

- *nan da* (literally "What?") indicates disappointment or even mild disgust.
- the ending *ya* implies resignation, and in this case is slightly derogatory.

A famous line from manga

From the series *Tensai Bakabon* ("Genius Bakabon"): Generally at the end of the episode, Bakabon's father concludes that the conflict that arose during the story has been satisfactorily resolved, and declares *Kore de ii no da.* Other characters in the story may still be wondering what to do, but for "Papa," it's all settled.

© Akatsuka Fujio / *Tensai Bakabon,* Kodansha

<u>Papa:</u> これ で いい のだ!!
Kore de ii no da!!
this with OK/good (explan.-is)
"And that's the way it should be!!"
(PL2)

Lesson 13 • *Yatta*, the exclamation

Yatta is the plain/abrupt past form of the verb *yaru* ("do"), so it basically means "I/he/you/they did it," and in fact, it can be used as a simple sentence meaning nothing more than that. But as the examples on these pages show, one of its most prominent uses is as an exclamation of joy. When the speaker or someone else has been able to accomplish a desired goal or task, it can combine the literal meaning of ". . . did it" with a feeling of "Hurray/All right!!/Yeah!/Wow!" Other times, it's used when a fortunate or lucky event has occurred, and it's pretty much pure "Hurray!/etc.," without the ". . . did it" meaning.

One of the reasons why we chose this topic for a Basic Japanese lesson is that this usage clearly differentiates the verbs *yaru* and *suru*, which both basically mean "do." In some cases the two are interchangeable (*yaru* is generally more informal), but the plain/abrupt past of *suru* (*shita*) doesn't work as an exclamation.

The other reason is that this is a simple, easy-to-pronounce word which can give your Japanese a spontaneous and colloquial-sound. These illustrations should give you a good feel for situations when you can sound like a native by coming out with a simple *Yatta*!

With the basic *banzai* position

He finally got a date: this man had been trying to get a date with the young lady on the right for some time. She finally agrees, and he raises his arms in celebration just as the fireworks go off.

Man: やったア! バンザーイ!!
Yattā Banzāi!!
"I did it! Hurray!!" (PL2)

Sound FX: ポン ポン ポーン
Pon pon pōn
(sound of fireworks going off)

- we translated *yatta* as "I did it!" partly to distinguish it from *banzai!!*, but as you can see in the examples that follow, *yatta* is often used like *banzai!!*/Hurray!!
- a small katakana ア is used to elongate *yatta* to *yattā*. He elongates the sound because he's shouting it out.

© Nagamatsu Kiyoshi / *Torao-san no O-ki ni Iri*, Kōdansha

They didn't really do anything

In these scenes the people saying *yatta* are more passive recipients than people who finally accomplished something through their own efforts.

This boy's father gave him a bicycle as a surprise gift. While he may have made his wish for a bicycle known and asked his father to get him one, this *yatta* seems to be more a simple exclamation of joy.

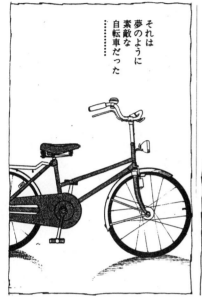

Narration: それ は 夢のように 素敵な 自転車 だった。
Sore wa yume no yō ni suteki-na jitensha datta.
that as-for like a dream (adv.) wonderful bicycle it was

"It was the kind of wonderful bicycle like you'd see in a dream." (PL2)

* *yume no yō ni* functions like an adverb modifying *suteki-na* ("wonderful/terrific/sharp-looking").

Boy: やったあ!
Yattā!
"Yea!"

* *yatta* is elongated to *yattā* here by adding a hiragana あ (*a*) at the end.

© Yajima & Hirokane / *Ningen Kōsaten*, Shogakukan

It's a drawing (福引き *fukubiki*) at a supermarket. The octagonal drum contains different colored balls, representing different prizes. To participate, you give it a turn and a ball comes out of a hole in the drum.

© Kobayashi Makoto / *What's Michael!?*, Kōdansha

Sound FX: ガラガラ
Gara gara
rattle rattle (balls tumbling in the drum)

Cat (clerk): おめでとうございます。5等、ビーフ味の ガムでーす。
Omedetō gozaimasu. go-tō, biifu-aji no gamu dēsu.
congratulations fifth-rank beef-flavored gum it is
"Congratulations. It's fifth prize, beef-flavored chewing gum." (PL3)

Dog (customer): やったー!
Yattā!
"All right!!" (PL2)

* the suffix *-tō* is used to designate ranking/grade. For example:
    一等国 (*ittō-koku*) = "first-class country" → "world power"
    一等車 (*ittō-sha*) = "first-class carriage/car" (on a train)
* *yatta* is elongated to *yattā* here with a wavy line.

A slightly exaggerated reaction

To most people, picking up a ¥100 coin would not be cause for such rejoicing, but this could well be the high point of the month for Tanaka-kun.

Tanaka-kun: あっ! 100円 めっけ!!
A! Hyaku-en mekke!!
"Aha! I found ¥100!!" (PL2)

- *mekke* is a colloquial contraction of *mitsuketa* (見つけた), the plain/abrupt past of *mitsukeru* (見つける "find") — not really slang, but an informal kind of word.

Tanaka-kun: やった! やったー! ラッキー!
Yatta! Yattā! Rakkii!
"All right! All right! I'm so lucky!" (PL2)

- *rakkii* is the English word "lucky" rendered in katakana, but this word has become quite popular and has taken on its own Japanese personality. This is typical usage.

© Tanaka Hiroshi / *Naku-na! Tanaka-kun,* Take Shobo

Examining their freshly fired pottery

These ceramic artists are obviously pleased with the results. They were using a method called 野焼き (*no-yaki,* literally "field baking") in which a huge bonfire is built over the pottery to be glazed.

Top right: わあっ!
Wā!
"Wow!"

Top left: ほほう。
Ho hō.
"Well, well!"

Lower right: できた、できた!
Dekita, dekita!
"It's done, it's done!"

Lower center: やったーっ!
Yattā!
"Yeah!"

Lower left: おおっ!
Ō!
"Aah!"

© Ueyama Tochi / *Cooking Papa,* Kōdansha

A reward for working late

It's past 7:30, and they are finally leaving the office, so this boss invites his employees out to eat. The employees had just been saying that the company should do something on their behalf since they were working so late.

Boss: どこか に 食事 に 行こうじゃないか。
Doko ka ni shokuji ni ikō ja nai ka?
somewhere to meal for let's go is it not that
"Why don't we go somewhere for dinner?"
(PL2)

Employees: エッ
E!
"What?"

© Gyū & Kondō / *Eigyō Tenteko Nisshi,* Scholar

Boss: これくらいは 会社の経費 で 認めてもらう ように 交渉してみる よ。
Kore kurai wa kaisha no keihi de mitomete morau yō ni kōshō shite miru yo.
this much company expense as have recognized so that (I'll) try negotiating (emph.)
"I'll see if I can't have that much recognized as a company expense." (PL2)

Employees: やったー!
Yattā!
"All right!"

Just like in the proverb

The golf course where this man works is being visited by a famous pro. Knowing of the pro's reputation as a stickler for neatness, he prepares for the visit with a thorough clean-up of the clubhouse, and succeeds in creating a good impression.

© Sakata & Kazama / *Kaze no Daichi,* Shogakukan

Ishihara: 相手 を 知れば 百戦 危うからず。
Aite o shireba hyaku-sen ayaukarazu.
other party (obj.) if know many battles not dangerous
"Know your opponent and be safe through a hundred battles." (PL2)

ヤッタ ね。
Yatta ne!
(I) did it didn't I
"I pulled it off, didn't I!" (PL2)

- *hyaku-sen* is written with the kanji for "hundred-battles," but it can be used to mean simply "many battles."
- *ayaukarazu* is a classical form of *abunakunai* ("not dangerous").

Yatta in sports scenes

In a sports setting, it's easy to think of *yatta* as "(I/they/someone) did it!" since there is a physical action involved; however, after the earlier examples, you can probably see at least some of the "Hurray!" aspect as well. In this scene, the impetuous young golfer (named Okita) decides to use a driver where the course pros recommend an iron.

SoundFX:
グシャッ
Gusha!
(sound of driver smacking golf ball)

© Sakata & Kazama / *Kaze no Daichi*, Shogakukan

© Sakata & Kazama / *Kaze no Daichi*, Shogakukan

<u>**Spectator 1:**</u> うおおっ! こりゃ 300 ヤード だーっ!!
Uō!   Korya sanbyaku yādo da—!!
(exclam.) this   300 yards   is
"Wow! That'll go 300 yards!!" (PL2)

<u>**Spectator 2:**</u> やったーっ!!
Yattā!!
"He did it!!" (PL2)

The golfer, Okita, also says *yatta* to himself (this is a continuation of the scene above). In this case, however, he is referring to the fact that he has finally managed to totally concentrate and shut out all external noise as he makes his shot.

He uses the politer (PL3) form *yarimashita* in announcing his accomplishment to the manager of the course (also a golfer), who thinks he is referring to his successfully pulling off the unconventional shot. The manager, a seasoned ex-pro, is being shown up by this young upstart, and it's starting to get on his nerves.

Okita:
やった!
Yattā!
"I did it!"
(PL2)

© Sakata & Kazama / *Kaze no Daichi*, Shogakukan

<u>**Okita:**</u>
やりましたっ、力石さん!
Yarimashita, Riseki-san!
"I did it, Riseki-san!" (PL3)

<u>**Riseki:**</u>
今さら   感心する 事じゃねえ よ。
Ima sara   kanshin suru koto ja nē   yo.
at this late stage be impressed thing is not (emph.)
"I'm not going to be impressed at this stage in the game." (PL1)

お前さん は ズーッと やりっ放し だ よ!
Omae-san wa zūtto yarippanashi da yo!
you   as-for all along nothing but doing it is/are(emph.)
"You've been doing it all day long!" (PL1-2)

Cheering a home run

From the series 鎌倉ものがたり (*Kamakura Monogatari*, "Kamakura Story"), by Nishigishi Ryōhei, perhaps better known as the creator of 三丁目の夕日 (*San-Chōme no Yūhi*, "Evening Sun of 3-Chōme").

Girl: ワー！　キャー！　やった やった! ホームラン！
Wā!　Kyā!　Yatta yatta!　Hōmuran!
(exclam.) (scream)　hurray hurray　(a) home run
"Wow! Oh boy! He did it, he did it! It's a home run!" (PL2)

Dog: ワンワン
wan wan
"Arf arf"

© Nishigishi Ryōhei / *Kamakura Monogatari*, Futabasha

Not exactly a sport, but . . .

This little old lady sneaks off from the family vegetable stand and plays pachinko whenever she can. Kōsuke came to tell her the shop was busy and they needed her help, but he gets caught up in the excitement and winds up playing himself.

Sound FX: スコン
Sukon
(sound of pachinko ball falling in the slot)

パピコン　パピコン
Papikon　papikon
(an electronic scoring sound, like a pinball machine)

Little Old Lady: やったあ!!
Yattā!!
I did it
"Aw'right!!" (PL2)

おまえ　福の神　だ　ね。
Omae fuku no kami da ne.
you　god of luck　are　aren't you
"You're a good luck charm, aren't you." (PL2)

Sound FX: チーン
Chiin
(chime-like sound as balls are released)

ジャラ　ジャラ　ジャラ
Jara　jara　jara
(sound of balls rolling out of machine)

© Maekawa Tsukasa / *Dai-Tōkyō Binbō Seikatsu Manyuaru*, Shogakukan

Lesson 14 • Saying "Goodbye"

Many ways of saying "goodbye" in Japanese are closely tied to the context. A good example is a pair of expressions used when a person leaves home: いってきます *itte kimasu* (literally "I will go and come," said by the person departing), and いっていらっしゃい *itte irasshai* (literally "[you] go and come," said by the person staying behind). These are also the appropriate "goodbyes" when an employee ducks out of the office for lunch, or when one leaves some other "home base" with the expectation of returning. In other situations they don't work.

Since we can't cover all of the possibilities in a single issue, we've decided to focus on two of the more common ways of saying "goodbye" that aren't so closely tied to context: さよなら *sayonara* (or more formally さようなら *sayōnara*), and the "*ja* (じゃ) group."

Sayō is the old/literary equivalent of *sono yō* ("that way/like that"), and *nara* means "if," so the underlying meaning of *sayōnara* is "if it's that way/if that's the case." *Ja* is a contraction of *de wa*, which means "in that case," so the basic meaning of both of these expressions is the same. That doesn't mean, however, that they're interchangeable in actual usage.

A note of finality

Sayonara is used much like the English "goodbye." If the parting is final, *sayonara* is a good choice, since one of the more common forms of the "*ja* group" implies that there will be a subsequent meeting.

In this scene, the woman is drinking as she recalls telling her boyfriend goodbye. He was in prison for injuring a man who was trying to attack her, but she decided she couldn't wait for him, and had to get on with her life. She has just told him she won't come to visit him anymore.

Woman: さよなら。
Sayonara.
"Good-Bye."

Sound FX: タッ
Ta!
(sound of foot
striking floor)

Sound FX: タッ タッ タッ
Ta! ta! ta!
(running foot-
steps)

© Yajima & Hirokane / *Ningen Kōsaten*, Shogakukan

Goodbye and good riddance

This young man has enrolled in a school for chefs. The head of the school tells him he must cut his hair if he wants to become a chef. He thinks she is bluffing, but when he refuses, she simply tells him "goodbye."

Student:　ケッ、やめたやめた。オレ は 帰る ぜっ。
Ke! Yameta yameta. Ore wa kaeru ze!
pshaw! (I) quit (I) quit I as-for go home (emph)
"That's it! I quit, I quit, I'm outta here." (PL2)

Teacher:　ハイ、さようなら グッバ〜〜イ。
Hai, sayōnara gubbāi.
"All right, goodbye, sayonara."

• *yameta* is the plain past of the verb *yameru* ("quit").

© Ueyama Tochi / *Cooking Papa*, Kōdansha

At the end of a TV program

© Urasawa Naoki / *Yawara!*, Shogakukan

The elderly gentleman on the screen is the grandfather of one of the contestants in a jūdō match which was being broadcast, but the voice is that of the announcer, off-screen. Announcers often use *sayōnara* at the end of a radio or TV program.

Announcer:　それ では 福岡国際センター から、さようなら!!
Sore de wa Fukuoka Kokusai Sentā kara, sayōnara!!
that with/at Fukuoka International Center from goodbye
"Then, from the Fukuoka International Center, goodbye!!"

Sound FX:　ブンチャカ ブンチャカ
Bunchaka bunchaka
(music—could be a march, or perhaps "cheerleading music," like drums and whistles.)

Not always final

These children are saying goodbye as they leave school for the day. In colloquial speech, *sayonara* is often pronounced as *sainara*, especially in the Kansai/Osaka dialect.

© Haruki Etsumi / *Jarinko-Chie*, Futabasha

1st child:　それじゃあ。
Sore jā.
Well then
"So long." (PL2)

2nd child:　うん、さいなら。
Un sainara.
"Uhm, g'bye."

3rd child:　さいなら。
Sainara.
"G'bye."

The complete *jā* expression

The short, informal expressions in the "*jā* group" are abbreviated forms of complete sentences like those in the following two frames.

© Saitō Takao / *Gorugo 13 Series,* Shogakukan

Kraus: それじゃあ また 明日 会おう。
Sore jā   mata   ashita   aō.
well then   again tomorrow let's meet
**"Well then, I'll see you again tomor-
row."** (PL2)

- *aō* is a plain/abrupt (PL2) version of *aimashō*
  ("let's meet"), from the verb *au* ("meet").

The complete salesman

© Torii Kazuyoshi / *Toppu Wa Ore Da!,* Shogakukan

Hikono: それじゃ また 明日 伺います!
Sore ja   mata   ashita   ukagaimasu!
well then   again   tomorrow (I) will call on you
"Well then, I'll call on you again tomorrow." (PL2)

FX: ペコリ ペコリ ペコリ
Pekori   pekori   pekori
(an adaptation of *peko peko*, the effect of bowing/being humble)

Sore ja in context

Sore ja is frequently used in a rather vague sense meaning "well then/in that case," but in this example, *sore* refers specifically to the housewife's headache ("In that case" → "Since you have a headache").

© Takahashi Rumiko / *P no Higeki,* Shogakukan

Housewife: ちょっと 私 頭痛 が...
Chotto   watashi   zutsū   ga
slightly   I   headache (subj.)
"I have a slight headache."

- *zutsū ga suru* = "have a headache."
  The *suru* is simply implied here.

Neighbor: あら、それ じゃ、
Ara,   sore   ja,
well/my that with/by
"Goodness, in that case,"

失礼する わね。
shitsurei suru   wa ne.
(I'll be impolite (fem. colloq.)
"I'll excuse myself."

Housewife: ほっ
ho!
(short sigh of relief)

- for more examples of the use of
  shitsurei when saying goodbye, see
  Lesson 11.

Short

More often than not, various parts of the sentence are left unsaid. The friend in this example stops with *mata* ("again"), and simply implies that they will meet again. Unlike the previous example, this *sore* doesn't refer to anything specific.

© Oze Akira / *Natsuko no Sake,* Kōdansha

Friend: それじゃ 夏子さん、また。
Sore ja   Natsuko-san mata.
well then   Natsuko   again
"Well then, Natsuko, I'll see you later." (PL2)

Natsuko: はい。
Hai.

Shorter

じゃね、また。
Ja ne   mata.
well   again
"Well, see you later."

© Matsumoto Reiji / *Kurimuzon Fō,* Shogakukan

Shortest

These OLs typically use very informal speech among themselves.

© Tsukamoto Tomoko / *Karā-na Ai,* Shogakukan

じゃ。
Ja.
"Well then."
(PL2)

Some possible permutations of the "*jā* group"

Just about any combination of *sore,* *jā* (or *ja*), *mata* and *ne* can be and is used, including:

sore de wa	*jā ne*	*jā, mata*
sore jā	*jā na* (masc.)	*mata ne/na*
hon jā		*jā, mata ne/na*
n jā		*jā ne/na, mata*

Three simple goodbyes

Each of these children uses a different style of goodbye, but all are common expressions.

Narration: るみちゃん は 帰っていった。
Rumi-chan wa kaette itta.
Rumi as for went home
Rumi went home. (PL2)

Rumi: じゃーねー！
Jā nē!
"So long!" (PL2)

Friend 1: バイバーイ！
Baibāi!
"Bye-bye!" (PL2)

Friend 2: またねー！
Mata nē!
"(See you) again!" (PL2)

- using a version of the English "bye-bye" or "good-bye" usually has a very informal and "cute" feel.

© Mori Masayuki / *Pokketo Sutōrii*, Kōdansha

On the phone

Ja is used on the phone just like it is in person.

Sound FX: カチャン
Kachan
(sound of hanging up phone)

Caller:
いい？ 今日 の 午後 でも？
Ii? Kyō no gogo de mo?
All right? today 's afternoon even
"(Is it) all right? (Maybe) even this afternoon?" (PL2)

じゃ。
Ja.
"Bye, then." (PL2)

- *shitsurei shimasu* is a more formal/polite way to end a phone conversation, and *gomen kudasai* is even more formal/polite.

© Saimon Fumi / *Asunaro Hakusho*, Shogakukan

A couple of older forms

In this story from the *Urusei Yatsura* series, Ataru has sprouted wings after Lum applies a strange medicine to his stiff shoulders. With this advantage he is able to outmaneuver his rival, Mendō.

© Takahashi Rumiko / *Urusei Yatsura,* Shogakukan

Ataru: さらば だ、わが 宿命 のライバル!
Saraba da waga shukumei no raibaru!
farewell (it) is my fate 's rival
"It's farewell, my fated rival!" (PL2)

Mendō: わー!
Wā!
"Yeow!"

- *saraba* comes from the old/literary form *sa araba,* which (like *sayonara*) means "if it is that way/in that case." Unlike *sayonara, saraba* still retains a literary feel, and using it in ordinary speech can give a dramatic and/or humorous tone.

This singer has come to meet his competition (Kōji) before a big singing contest. He vows to "crush" him in the contest, and leaves with this dramatic line.

Haneda: あばよ...コージ。
Abayo ... Kōji.
"So long ... Kōji."

- several theories exist concerning the origin of *abayo.* One suggests that it is a contraction of *sa araba* plus the emphatic *yo.* Both *saraba* and *abayo* are used mostly by males.

© Tsuchida Seiki / *Orebushi,* Shogakukan

There are many other expressions which can be used as a kind of "goodbye."

Ki o tsukete
"Be careful/Take care." Typically used when the other person has to travel home.

Genki de ...
"[Be] in good health." Usually said when there will be a long absence, or when the parting is final.

O-daiji ni ...
"Take good care [of yourself]." Generally used when the other person is not in good health.

O-jama shimashita
"I intruded on you." Said when leaving someone's home, office, etc.

Oitoma shimasu
"I'll take my leave." An old-fashioned touch: also used in variations such as *Mō o-itoma shinakereba narimasen.*

O-saki ni (shitsurei shimasu) ↔ *Otsukare-sama (deshita)*
"(Excuse me) [for leaving] ahead of you." Said when leaving the workplace while others are still remaining, no matter how late the hour. ↔ *Otsukare-sama is* basically a "thank you" for working hard — *tsukare* is from the verb *tsukareru* ("become tired") and is used as "goodbye" by the others who are staying behind. Another equally untranslatable variation is *Gokurō-sama (deshita),* in which *kurō* means "toils/hard labors."

Dōmo
This all-purpose word can be used as an abbreviated form of several other expressions for "goodbye" (see Lesson 8).

Lesson 15 • The Concept of *Komaru*

The kanji for *komaru* 困 represents a tree 木 pent up inside a box 口, which gives an effective graphic image of the word's basic meaning: to be caught in a tight spot. That's a universal experience, of course, but the range of tight spots covered by the single word *komaru* may be a surprise. It can refer to becoming distressed/troubled/inconvenienced, being in need/want of something, being perplexed or at a loss about what to do or simply being embarrassed. It can also be an open expression of dismay/objection/refusal when one has been asked to do something not on the up-and-up.

With so many possibilities, *komaru* is another one of those words you basically just have to get a "feel" for by hearing it used — or seeing it in manga! It's worth noting, though, that the present and past forms of the verb tend to carry different implications: *komaru/komarimasu* often implies that the speaker's distress is the other person's fault or responsibility, while *komatta/komarimashita* is usually more of a "no-fault" expression of personal distress. Sometimes a distinction is made between ongoing situations (*komaru*), and specific events (*komatta*). But even these very general distinctions can be altered by the context, so once again, we let the examples speak. They don't cover all of the possibilities, but they should give you a pretty good idea what to say the next time you feel like a tree inside a box.

Obviously distressed

This reluctant sumō trainee is being fattened up by his trainer. He wants to stay slim so he can get a date with a girl in his neighborhood, but his mother wants him to become a famous *sumō* wrestler.

© Akatsuka Fujio / *Gyagu-ya*, Kōdansha

Trainer: もっと 太る んだ。
Motto futoru n da.
more   get fat (command)
"You will gain more weight!"

Matsutarō: ゲゲーッ! 困る んだ よーっ!!
Ge gē! Komaru n da yo—!!
aargh (I) will be distressed (explan.) (emph.)
"Aargh! You can't do this to me!!"

- *n da*, a contraction of *no da*, is typically used to indicate that an explanation is being made, but in a very broad sense. In the first sentence, the trainer is "explaining" that the boy <u>will</u> gain more weight, i.e., it's used as a command. In the second sentence, the boy is "explaining" that he will not be happy if they pour that big pot of *chanko nabe* down his throat.

A perplexing situation

The young man on the left is a straight-arrow salesman for an appliance maker. The middle-aged man on the right is the owner of an appliance store. He has lost money playing the stock market and is unable to pay the appliance maker for the last shipment, so he offers a bribe to the salesman to help him cover up the situation.

Yōsuke: こ、これ は...
Ko, kore wa . . .
th, this (subj.)
"Wh, what's this?"

Maebatake: ま、ちょっとしたお小遣い ぐらい だ が ね。
Ma, chotto shita o-kozukai gurai da ga ne.
well slight pocket change only is but (colloq.)
"Well, it's just a little pocket change." (PL2)

Yōsuke: こ こまります!
Ko, komarimasu!
"I, I can't accept this!"

- *gurai* (or *kurai*) can mean "about/approximately," but here it means "just/only."

© Gyū & Kondō / *Eigyō Tenteko Nisshi,* Scholar

Stuck on a bus in heavy traffic

These passengers are wondering if they should just get off and walk.

Sound FX: パー パー パー パー
Pā pā pā pā
(sound of horns blowing)

FX: のろ のろ のろ
Noro noro noro
(effect of moving slowly)

Passenger: ふーむ
Fu—mu
"Hmmm" (wondering what to do)

Kōsuke: 困っちゃうなあ。
Komatchau nā.
(thinking) **"This is terrible."** (PL2)

- *komatchau* is a contraction of *komatte shimau.* When the verb *shimau* is added to other verbs it can give the meaning "completely/thoroughly."

© Maekawa Tsukasa / *Dai Tōkyō Binbō Seikatsu Manyuaru,* Kōdansha

Using *komaru* to say "You must . . ."

There is an important meeting back at the office, but he is off to the race track. She is trying to get him to go back with her but he is resisting. In this scene she is blocking the door to the subway train.

© Kariya & Hanasaki / *Oishinbo*, Shogakukan

Kurita: 来てくださらないと 困ります。
Kite kudasaranai to komarimasu.
if you do not come   it will be a problem
"You've got to come." (PL2)

- *kite* is from the verb *kuru* ("come").
- *kudasaru* after a verb gives the meaning "do for me/us," with a humble tone. She is using the negative form, *kudasaranai*.
- after a verb, the particle *to* gives a conditional "if" meaning. It is a negative conditional + *komaru* that makes the meaning of "must."

Using *komaru* to say "You must not . . ."

This woman wants a grandchild as soon as possible, but her son and daughter-in-law are having trouble complying. The daughter-in-law is going to a cooking school to learn how to prepare foods that will increase their chances of producing an heir for the family, and the prospective grandmother is telling her to take her studies seriously.

Mother-in-law: しかし　　遊び半分　　では
Shikashi asobi-hanbun de wa
but   half for fun   if it is
困ります　　　　　　よ、奈可子さん!
komarimasu   yo, Nakako-san!
(I) will be distressed (emph.)   Nakako
"But it won't do for you to take it lightly, now, Nakako." (PL3)

- *asobi* is a noun form of the verb *asobu* ("play/have fun/enjoy oneself"), and *hanbun* means "half." *Asobi-hanbun* means that a seriousness of purpose is lacking.

© Nishi & Hashimoto / *Fūfu Seikatsu*, Shogakukan

There is a big exhibition coming up for food products, and this man has been asked to give up some of the space he had reserved. He's obviously not willing.

Businessman: バカ　　　言っちゃ　　　困る　　　よッ!
Baka   itcha   komaru   yo!
foolishness if (you) say (I) will be distressed (emph.)
"Don't talk nonsense!" (PL2)

Sign: 安元　　　　食品
Yasumoto shokuhin
Yasumoto Foods

- *itcha* is a contraction of *itte wa*, from the verb *iu* ("say").

© Hijiri Hideo / *Dakara Shōsuke*, Shogakukan

Present vs. past tense

All of the examples so far have used the present form of *komaru*. We'll now look at some examples using the past form. Although there are generalizations which can be made concerning the use of present vs. past, the choice sometimes seems almost arbitrary. Here's one example.

Money problems:
The man on the right, Doronuma, is in a financial bind. Unable to pay back his loan to a finance company, he asks for an extension, but he must come up with a co-signer. The man on the left is Haibara, the finance company agent.

In the first scene, Haibara is directly involved with the problem — if Doronuma can't repay the loan or find a co-signer, Haibara is in trouble too. Haibara teaches Doronuma a method of buying long distance train tickets with a credit card and reselling them to discount travel agencies. Doronuma pays off the finance company this way, but he now owes the credit card company even more money.

Doronuma plans to pay off the credit card with his bonus, but in the second scene, he has realized he won't get much of a bonus, so he's back looking for another loan. Haibara's surprise is feigned — he could have guessed that Doronuma was getting in deeper and deeper.

The name Doronuma literally means "mud-swamp," and Haibara means "ash-plain."

© Aoki Yūji / *Naniwa Kinyūdō*, Kōdansha

Doronuma: もう 保証人 を 頼める 知りあい は いない んです。
Mō hoshōnin o tanomeru shiriai wa inai n desu.
now guarantor (obj.) can request acquaintance as-for there is not (explan.)
"There is no one I can ask to co-sign." (PL3)

Haibara: そうですか。困りましたねー。
Sō desu ka. Komarimashita ne–.
"Is that so. That's a problem, isn't it." (PL3)

© Aoki Yūji / *Naniwa Kinyūdō*, Kōdansha

Doronuma: ボーナス が ほとんど 出ない んです わ。
Bōnasu ga hotondo denai n desu wa.
bonus (subj.) almost will not be paid (explan.) (emph.)
"I'll get almost no bonus." (PL3)

Haibara: エッ それ は 困る じゃないですか。 どうする つもり です か！
E! Sore wa komaru ja nai desu ka. Dō suru tsumori desu ka?!
huh! that as-for is troubling is it not do what intention is (?)
"Huh! That puts you in a tight situation, doesn't it. What do you intend to do?" (PL3)

Another mix of past and present forms

She is a reporter at a major Tōkyō newspaper. A very wealthy (and very handsome) businessman she had recently interviewed calls to ask her out to dinner. She doesn't want to go, but is at a loss as to how to refuse. Her co-worker can't understand why she would even hesitate.

Kurita: あ、あの ちょっと お待ち ください。
A, ano   chotto   o-machi   kudasai.
Uuh   little   waiting   please (give)
"U, uuh, can you wait just a minute?" (PL3)

困った　　　わ、
Komatta   wa,
(I'm) troubled (fem.)

また 食事 に 誘われて しまって。
mata shokuji ni sasowarete shimatte.
again meal to being invited (regret)

**"This is awkward. I've been asked out to dinner
again."** (PL2)

Co-worker: 困る　　　　こと　　ない　でしょ!
Komaru   koto   nai   desho!
become troubled thing there is not is there
"There's nothing awkward about it, is there?"
(PL2)

- Kurita <u>has become</u> troubled by the invitation, so the past form, *komatta*, seems natural. Her co-worker is saying that there is no reason <u>to become</u> troubled.

© Kariya & Hanasaki / *Oishinbo*, Shogakukan

It's a scam

This man is an *atari-ya* (当たり屋), a person who fakes accidents for the purpose of extortion. He will claim that being incapacitated will prevent him from completing a business deal that would have made him £50,000. The "doctor" is his accomplice.

"Doctor": そうですねえ 全治　三か月...
Sō desu nē   zenchi   sankagetsu
let's see   full cure three months

いや、それ 以上 かかる 可能性 も...
iya   sore   ijō   kakaru kanōsei mo...
no   that more than take possibility also

**"Well, let's see, three months for complete re-
covery . . . No, it's even possible it could take
longer than that . . ."** (PL2)

"Victim": いやあ、困りました。
Iyā   komarimashita.
(excl.)   (I'm) troubled
**"Well, this puts me in a
real bind."** (PL2)

© Katsuhika & Urusawa / *Master Kiiton*, Shogakukan

Komatta as a modifier

A group of reporters has been invited to the opening of a huge new department store with a fresh food section in the lower level and a restaurant floor on top. Super-cynic reporter Yamaoka is not impressed, and is shown here walking out after making disparaging remarks about the quality of the restaurants and the freshness of the food.

Reporter 1: 板山　会長　を　怒らせる　とは...
Itayama kaichō　o　okoraseru　to wa...
(name)　chairman (obj.) make angry　the idea of
"Making Chairman Itayama mad . . ." (PL2)

Reporter 2: 東西さん　も　困った　こと　になる　ぜ。
Tōzai-san　mo　komatta　koto　ni naru　ze.
(name-hon.)　also　troubled　situation　will become　(emph.)
"It'll mean trouble for the Tōzai too!"

- *okoraseru* is the causative form of the verb *okoru* ("become angry").
- Tōzai is the name of the newspaper where this impetuous reporter works. It's not unusual for the *-san* ending to be used with a company name, just as it is with a person's name.

Just plain *komatta*

In this scene, Shima-kachō is trying to figure out how he will tell a business associate that his girlfriend is actually a married woman.

Shima-kachō: 困ったな . . .
Komatta na . . .
"How am I going to do this?" (PL2)

© Hirokane Kenshi / *Kachō Shima Kōsaku*, Kōdansha

Lesson 16 • Counters and Classifiers

Counters and classifiers are used to a certain extent even in English — for example, we refer to "three <u>sheets</u> of paper," or "eight <u>head</u> of cattle" — but counters in Japanese take on a far greater importance. There are counters for small animals, large animals, birds, flat objects, cylindrical objects, cars, planes, boats, ships, suits, pistols, pairs of chopsticks, and so on, some might say *ad nauseum*. Formidable as this may seem at first, learning these counters and using them properly can be a source of satisfaction as one works toward fluency. On the other hand, for the fainthearted it's reassuring to know that there are generic counters (*hitotsu, futatsu, mittsu*, etc.), which will at least enable you to be understood if you need a counter but don't know which one to use.

Unintentional "bloopers" by the inexperienced sometimes lead to knee-slapping results, but, as some of our examples show, counters can also be misused deliberately for humorous effect. When the humor you generate with your counters becomes fully intentional, you know you have arrived.

Even after you get used to the sheer number and variety of counters in Japanese, it can be surprising just how wide a range some of the counters can cover. Since we can't begin to do justice to the number and variety of counters in these few pages, we've decided to devote this lesson mostly to –*hon* 本, which is one of the counters with the widest range of meanings.

By itself, the kanji 本 can mean either "book" or "origin," and as a prefix it means "main-/this-," but as a counter/classifier it's used for things that are cylindrical or that have a long, thin shape. In our first three examples, these characteristics are obvious in the physical appearance of the objects, but in the others the characteristics are more abstract. For example, telephone calls and home runs are among the things counted with –*hon* because they both have qualities that could be considered "long and thin."

As with many counters, the reading –*hon* changes to –*bon* or –*ppon* in some combinations, for the sake of euphony. For example, *ichi + hon = ippon*.

The most basic usage of –*hon*

Daikon **radishes** are cylindrical in shape, so naturally they are counted with *hon*—*ippon, nihon, sanbon*, etc.

© Irie Kiwa / *Haikibun Sakana-hime*, Kōdansha

Woman: 大根　1本　ちょーだい。
Daikon ippon cho~dai.
radish　one　please give me
"One *daikon*, please." (PL2)

Vendor: アイヨ　　葉っぱ は?
Ai yo Happa wa?
OK (emph.)　leaves　as-for
"Coming up. How about the leaves?"

Woman: その まま。
Sono mama.
as is
"Leave them on."

Sign: みやちゃん の 八百屋
Miya-chan no yaoya
"Miya's Vegetable Market"

• *chōdai* is used like *kudasai*, but has a softer sound. Although *chōdai* is more typically used by women, it's not uncommon for men to use it in certain situations.
• *ai* is a colloquial form of *hai* ("Yes ma'am/sir").

Counting golf clubs

Only three clubs? You would expect *a buchō* ("department head") who is also a golf enthusiast to have a full set of clubs, but Akai-buchō claims that three clubs are enough for "man's golf" (*otoko no gorufu*). He claims the clubs are worth over ¥1,000,000 each.

© Wakabayashi Kenji / *Heisei Arashiyama Ikka,* Shogakukan

Arashiyama: あら？　赤井部長 . . .
Ara?　Akai-buchō . . .
(exclam.)　(name-title)
"What? Mr. Akai . . ."

3本　　しか　持ってないんです　か、クラブ？
san-bon shika motte-nai n desu ka, kurabu?
three　other than　don't have　is it that (?)　club(s)
"you only have three clubs?"

- *ara* is a typically feminine expression of surprise.
- the title *buchō* is used here with a name, as a substitute for *–san.* Since she is an employee of the same company, it might sound overly familiar, or slightly disrespectful to use *–san.*
- this is an example of "inverted syntax." The normal word order would be *Kurabu sanbon shika motte-nai n desu ka?*

Cat whiskers

This old man makes fishing lures (毛ばり, *kebari*) using cats' whiskers, but because of his age he has a hard time catching the cats. He demonstrates one of his lures to a young boy who eagerly agrees to a swap — 1,000 cat whiskers for one of the man's lures.

© Wakabayashi Kenji / *Sasaguchi-gumi,* Kōdansha

Old Man: 猫　の　ヒゲ　1000本　と　交換！
Neko no hige senbon to kōkan!
cat　('s) whisker(s)　1000　for　exchange
"A swap for 1000 cats' whiskers!"

というのは　どうじゃ？
To iu no wa dō ja?
saying that　how　is
"How about that?"

- *to iu no wa* refers back to what was said in the previous sentence or part of the sentence.
- *ja* is typically used by older males (and in some dialects) as a substitute for *da/desu.*

© Maekawa Tsukasa / *Dai-Tōkyō Binbō Seikatsu Manyuaru*, Kōdansha

Videotapes

The student who lives next door is away for a week at a *gasshuku* (合宿, "retreat/training session"), so Kōsuke borrows his TV and VCR and holds his own *bideo gasshuku* ("video retreat"). Movies (the physical film, as well as the story that's on it) are counted with –*hon* because of the long and thin shape of the film. The same practice naturally applies to videotapes, but with video disks, the disk itself is counted with –*mai* (for flat objects) while the movie/story is still counted with -*hon*.

Narration: 合宿　の　1週間　に　60本　以上　の　ビデオ　を　見続ける。
Gasshuku no isshūkan ni rokujuppon ijō no bideo o mitsuzukeru.
retreat ('s) one week during 60 more than of video(s) (obj) continue to watch
"During the one week retreat, I watched over 60 videos, one after the other."

- *gasshuku* are most typically training sessions for school sports "clubs" or teams.
- *mitsuzukeru* is a combination of the verbs *miru* ("see/watch") and *tsuzukeru* ("continue").

Telephone calls

He was delayed at work, and was over an hour late for a date, but neglected to call his girlfriend at the coffee shop where they were to meet. When he arrived, all he found was a note. Here, he is reflecting on his negligence.

Ibashi: せめて　電話の一本　も　入れればよかった　な。
Semete denwa no ippon mo irereba yokatta na.
at least one phone call even should have made (colloq)
"I should have at least given her a call."

今月,　一回　も　会わなかったもんな。
Kongetsu ikkai mo awanakatta mon na.
this month once even didn't meet (colloq)
"I didn't see her even one time this month."

- *denwa o ireru* is one way to say "make a phone call," similar to the English "put in a call." *Irereba* is the conditional form of the verb *ireru*, and *Irereba yokatta* literally means "It would have been good/better if I had made (a call)."
- *mon na* at the end of the second sentence is a contraction of *mono na*. *Mono* is used this way when explaining a situation.
- the telephone itself, as a small "machine," is counted with –*dai* (*ichidai, nidai, sandai*, etc.), but telephone calls are counted with –*hon*.
- *ikkai* is from *ichi* ("one") + *kai*, the counter for "times/occasions."

© Abe & Kurata / *Aji Ichimon Me*, Shogakukan

A counter double header

The counter *–hon* is used twice in this example, once in the literal sense (for referring to a one-legged batting stance), and once in a figurative sense (for counting home runs). The setting is an amateur baseball game in which a player suddenly takes on the persona of the Giants' Ō Sadaharu. The next day, Ō reveals that he had a dream about playing in an amateur game.

© Saigan Ryōhei / *Kamakura Monogatari*, Futabasha

Morita: あっ 関根さん あの 構え は!!
A! Sekine-san ano kamae wa!
"Ah, Sekine-san, that stance!!"

Sekine: そうです そうです。
Sō desu sō desu.
"That's right, that's right."

あの 王さんの 一本足 打法 ですよ。
Ano Ō-san no ippon-ashi dahō desu yo.
"It's Ō's one-legged batting style."

Narration: 王 貞治、
Ō Sadaharu,

不滅 の ホームラン 記録 868本、
fumetsu no hōmuran kiroku happyaku-rokujūhappon,
unbeatable (=) home run record 868-(count)
unbeatable record of 868 home runs,

国民 栄誉賞 の スーパースター。
kokumin eiyoshō no sūpāsutā.
national population honor award (=) superstar
the superstar who won the National Medal of Distinction.

Jūdō matches

A young jūdō athlete, out for a run, sees two cats fighting and steps in to referee.

Michael (the cat): ニャア～ッ
Nyaa~!
"Meoow!"

Sound FX: バァーン
Bān
(sound of cat hitting the ground; generic "pow/bang" loud sound)

"Referee": 一本!!
Ippon
"*Ippon*!!"

それ まで～。
Sore made~.
that until
"End of match."

• the term *ippon* is used in jūdō circles, even in English, to signify that the match has been won. It is scored as ten points.

© Kobayashi Makoto / *What's Michael?*, Kōdansha

Conventional use of *–hiki*

Small animals are counted using *–hiki* as shown in this first illustration. In the bottom two illustrations, however, *–hiki* is used to count men, giving a humorous effect.

© Okazaki Jiro / *Hitozaru no yu*, Shogakukan

These monkeys
live in the mountains near a hot spring. The man telling this story is searching for a friend who, disillusioned with human society, has disappeared. Could he have changed himself into a monkey?

<u>Narration:</u> その中の　　　一匹　が...
Sono naka no ippiki ga...
among those one-animal (subj.)
"One of them . . ."

<u>Narration:</u> 私の　　　顔　を　見て...
Watashi no kao o mite...
my   face (obj.) looked at, and
"looked at my face and . . ."

Humorous use of *–hiki*

© Tanioka Yasuji / *Bakuhatsu Suzen*, KK Best Book

A flirtatious wink affects this young man more than the girl in the neighboring train expected. Here he prepares to jump from his train to hers.

<u>Man:</u> 男　　　一匹!! ウインク に　かけて、　　　セーノセーノ
Otoko ippiki !! uinku ni kakete, sēno, sēno,
man   one   wink   on   staking it   (preparing to make effort)
"One man!! Staking it all on a wink, one-two, one-two . . ."

<u>FX:</u> ガタガタ
gata gata   (effect of leg trembling)

She seems to be enjoying having her husband jump the fence instead of the usual sheep.

<u>Kuriko:</u> 陽一さん　が 10匹、陽一さん　が　　11匹...
Yōichi-san ga juppiki, Yōichi-san ga jū-ippiki...
Yōichi (subj.) ten Yōichi (subj.) eleven
"Ten Yōichis, eleven Yōichis . . ."

<u>Yōichi:</u> ヒツジ にして　くれ　よ。
Hitsuji ni shite kure yo.
sheep   make it (request) (emph.)
"Make it sheep, will you." (PL2)

© Terashima Reiko / *Kuriko-san Konnichi wa*, Take Shobo

Conventional use of –*ko*

He has just eaten one of the five freshly-made croquettes he bought, and he knows that they will taste better if he waits a little before having another, but unable to resist, he has two in a row.

© Maekawa Tsukasa / *Dai-Tōkyō Binbō Seikatsu Manyuaru*, Kōdansha

Kōsuke: ガマン　　　　　　しきれず
        Gaman　　　　　　*shikerezu*
        endurance/perseverance unable to do/sustain
        "Unable to hold back,

        たて　　　続け　に　2個目　も　食べた。
        tate　　*tsuzuke ni niko-me mo tabeta.*
        immediate succession in second one also ate
        I ate the second one right after the first."

- *gaman suru* = "restrain oneself/endure," and *shikerezu* is a negative continuing form meaning "unable to completely . . ."
- the suffix –*me* is used to designate items in a series; so, *ikko-me* = "the first one," *niko-me* = "the second one," etc.

Humorous use of –*ko*

From the series *Urusei Yatsura*, Ataru inadvertently summons an interstellar taxi and rides it home from school, racking up a bill equivalent to all of the petroleum on earth. His father, unable to put up with the resulting pandemonium, considers swapping the entire earth for a ride to another planet. To show the insignificance of the earth on the interplanetary scale, it's referred to with the counter –*ko*, as if it were an orange or croquette.

© Takahashi Rumiko / *Urusei Yatsura*, Shogakukan

Father: 運転手さん、
      Untenshu-san,
      "Driver,

      地球　　一個分　　で　どのくらい　飛べる　んだ　ね!!
      chikyū ikko-bun de dono kurai toberu n da ne!!
      earth 1-(count)'s worth with about how much can fly(explan-?) (colloq.)
      how far can you take me for one Earth?"

"Driver": 地球　一個分　ねえ...
       Chikyū ikkobun nē...
       "One Earth's worth, hmmm . . ."

Sound FX: パチ　パチ　パチ
       Pachi pachi pachi
       (Sound of punching keys on calculator)

We don't have room to illustrate any more of the counters/classifiers, but here's a list of some of the more common ones.

- –*chō* 丁 blocks (of tōfu), orders (of a dish, in a restaurant)
- –*chō* 挺 pairs (of scissors)
- –*dai* 台 machines, typewriters, pianos, beds, cars, etc.
- –*hai* 杯 cupfuls, glassfuls, boxfuls, etc.
- –*jō* 畳 tatami mats
- –*ken* 軒 houses, shops, buildings
- –*ki* 機 airplanes
- –*nin* 人 persons
- –*mei* 名 persons (more formal than –*nin*)
- –*sara* 皿 plate(fuls)
- –*mai* 枚 flat things (empty plates)
- –*satsu* 冊 books, magazines
- –*wa* 羽 birds
- –*zen* 膳 bowls (of rice), pairs (of chopsticks)

If it's any consolation, keep in mind that Japanese uses the single word *mure* (群) to refer to a "herd" of cows, "flock" of sheep, "school" of fish, "bevy" of quail, "gaggle" of geese, etc.

Lesson 17 • Baby Talk

Although it doesn't come up in everyday conversation (unless you're a baby), it's nice to know a little about baby talk to see how native speakers progress in their use of Japanese. The examples that we show here fall into two categories.

- Words used only by or to children as substitutes for ordinary adult words:
  manma instead of *gohan* for "food/a meal,"
  nenne suru instead of *neru* for "sleep/go to bed,"
  an'yo instead of *ashi* for "foot/feet."

- Children's mispronunciation of adult words (like *hochii* instead of *hoshii*).
  As you will see in our examples, this change from "s" or "sh" sounds to "ch" is the most prominent mispronunciation. Although it's hard to say how accurately this reflects the way children actually talk, it is a convention used by adults to represent "baby talk."

Other characteristics of baby talk, or children's language, include:

- More frequent use of *no* as a sentence ending for both statements and questions.
- More frequent use of *yo* sentence endings (i.e., dropping *da/desu*).
- Heavier use of the honorific *o–* prefix, even when referring to one's own actions or possessions. This results from the parents (especially mothers) using such speech to their children. In this case, it's perhaps more of a diminutive, like adding "nice . . ./nice little . . ." in English when speaking to children. (Beware: some Japanese people seem to overuse polite speech when talking with foreign students of Japanese, especially beginners.)

We'll start with some of the more widely-used children's words.

Wan (wan)-chan

Wan wan is the ordinary Japanese equivalent of "bow wow/arf arf" in English. The ending *–chan* is a diminutive version of *–san*, added to people's names. *Wan-chan* is used even by older children and adults as a friendly way of referring to a dog (very similar to "doggie"), but *wan wan-chan* is definitely baby talk, perhaps something like calling a dog a "bow wow."

© Kobayashi Makoto / *What's Michael?*, Kōdansha

Tamami: ワンワン!!　ワンワン
wan-wan　　*wan-wan*
"Bow wow!! Bow wow"

Mother: そう　　　よ〜!! あれ は ワンワンちゃん よ!!
Sō　　　*yo–* *Are wa wan-wan-chan yo!!*
that's right (emph.) that as-for　doggie　(emph.)
"That's right! It's a bow wow (doggie)!!"

- the mother uses the emphatic particle *yo* like a verb, or, you could say that she has dropped the verb *da/desu*. This is a characteristic of informal feminine speech, and is not necessarily baby talk.

Bū bū

Looking out a bus window at all the traffic, this toddler (named Tamebō) uses a children's word which, like *wan-wan*, is also an ordinary sound effect used by adults as well as children. Using it this way (as a noun, "vehicle"), however, is definitely baby talk.

© Hosono Fujihiko / *MaMa,* Shogakukan

<u>**Tomebō:**</u>　ぶーぶー　ぶーぶー!
Bu– bu–　bu– bu–!
"Honk-honk, honk-honk!"

<u>**Hagiwara:**</u>　うん, ぶーぶー　いっぱい　ねー。
Un　bu–bu–　ippai　ne–.
"Uh-huh, there're lots of honk-honks, aren't there." (PL2)

- *ippai* can mean "full," or "lots of."

Nenne

The man lying on the floor is the managing director (*jōmu*) of Kanemaru Industries. He is playing with his friend's daughter.

© Ueyama Tochi / *Cooking Papa,* Kōdansha

<u>**Momoko:**</u>　じゃあ ねんね しましょうね。
Jā　nen-ne　shimashō ne.
"Now, let's go beddie-bye/night-night, okay?"

よし　よし。
Yoshi yoshi.
"There, there."

- like the verb *neru, nenne suru* can refer to sleeping or going to bed/lying down.
- *yoshi* literally means "good," or "OK."

Manma

Mother is ill, so Dad has taken over the care and feeding of the baby. This particular baby happens to be the reincarnation of a tough *yakuza* gangster.

© Tomisawa Chinatsu / *Teyandei Baby,* Kōdansha

<u>**Father:**</u>　サァ、星くん　マンマ でちゅよ〜。
Sā,　Hoshi-kun manma　dechu yo–.
"OK, Hoshi, it's din-din!"

<u>**Sound FX:**</u>　トン
Ton
(sound of plopping the baby down in the chair)

<u>**Hoshi-kun:**</u>　い...いい!!
I-　ii!!
"N–, No!!"

- *manma* is the baby talk equivalent of *gohan* (as used to mean "food/a meal").
- *dechu* is the baby talk distortion of the verb *desu*. More examples of this kind of mispronunciation are given on the following pages.

Hoshii → hochii

In the world of manga, the *shi* sound is hard for children to make, and with very young children it typically comes out as *chi*. Our more linguistically-enlightened colleagues tell us that in the languages of the world, the "s" sound is more common by far than the "ch" sound, and that phonetically, such a substitution is unlikely. No matter what the case, in the world of manga, TV comedy, etc., this substitution is perhaps the most common way of giving speech that infantile touch.

> **Tomebō:** いちごヨーグルト ほちー。
> *Ichigo yōguruto hochii–.*
> **"I want some strawberry yogurt."**

- *hoshii* is an adjective used to describe the object wanted.

© Hosono Fujihiko / *MaMa*, Shogakukan

Moshi moshi → mochi mochi

We don't know her exact age, but she might be a little older than Tomebō (above), who is two.

> **Megumi:** もち もち!
> *Mochi mochi!*
> **"Hello!"**

- *moshi moshi* is the standard phrase for "hello" on the phone.

© Yajima & Hirokane / *Ningen Kōsaten*, Shogakukan

Itashimashite → itachimachite

Resentful of the presence of this friend of his mother, Tomebō seems a little overly polite. The actual expression here is *Dō itashimashite.*

© Hosono Fujihiko / *MaMa*, Shogakukan

> **Tomebō:** ど! いたちまちてー。
> *Do itachimachite–.*
> **"Not at all/You're welcome."**

Sumō → chumō

Some sumō wrestlers are visiting the kindergarten to help make *mochi* rice cakes for a New Year's celebration.

> **FX:** おず おず
> *Ozu ozu*
> (effect of the boy's hesitance/apprehension)
> **Boy:** おちゅもうちゃん。
> *Ochumō-chan.*
> **"Mr. Sumō Wrestler."**

- this also illustrates how the honorific *–san* becomes *–chan* in baby talk.

© Ichimaru / *Okami-san*, Shogakukan

Jitensha → jitencha

The *sha* sound is a combination of *shi* and *ya*, so when the *shi* becomes *chi*, *sha* becomes *cha* (a combination of *chi* and *ya*).

Hagiwara: これ は ね、 自転車 っていう の!
kore wa ne jitensha tte iu no
this as-for (colloq.) bicycle called (explan.)
"(You) call this a *jitensha*." → **"This is called a bicycle!"** (PL2)

Tomebō: じてんちゃあーっ。
Jitenchā–!
"Jitenchā—?"

• in this and the example below, *tte iu no* is the equivalent of *to iu no (desu)*. Here, the verb *iu* means "call/refer to."

© Hosono Fujihiko / *MaMa,* Shogakukan

Kaerimashō → kaerimachō

The *sho* sound is a combination of *shi* and *yo*, so when the *shi* becomes *chi*, *sho* becomes *cho* (a combination of *chi* and *yo*).

Tomebō: かえりまちょ〜〜、マーマー!!
Kaerimacho– Ma–ma–!!
"Let's go home, Mama!!"

Mother: まーってなさい っていう の!
Ma–tte-nasai tte iu no!
wait (command) say that (explan.)
"(I'm telling you to) hold on!"

• *matte-(i)nasai* is from the verb *matsu* ("wait"). This is a gentle command form of *matte-iru*, the "progressive" form — she wants him to "be waiting" for some period of time while she finishes her shopping.
• in this case, the verb *iu* means "say/tell."

© Hosono Fujihiko / *MaMa,* Shogakukan

Itsu → Ichu

The *tsu* sound is one of the more difficult in the Japanese language, so it's not surprising that children would have trouble with it.

Father: めぐみ!
(name)
"Megumi!"

Megumi: パパ、いちゅも 遅い の ね。
Papa, ichumo osoi no ne.
daddy always late (explan) (colloq)
"Daddy, you're always late (coming home)."
(PL2)

© Yajima & Hirokane / *Ningen Kōsaten,* Shogakukan

"Me" in the third person?

Children often use their own names to refer to themselves. This child's name is Tometarō, but he's called Tomebō for short. He is infatuated with his kindergarten teacher, Machiko (given name), and in this scene he is announcing that he intends to marry her. (*O*)*yome*(*-san*) is a polite word for "bride," and (*o*)*yome ni naru* (literally "become a bride") is one way to refer to (a woman's) getting married. His misuse of this expression and his mispronunciation of *–san* as *–tan* generate some chuckles in this scene.

© Hosono Fujihiko / *MaMa*, Shogakukan

Tomebō: トメボーね、トメボーね、
Tomebō ne Tomebō ne
まちこセンセーの およめたん に なる のー。
Machiko-sensē no oyome-tan ni naru no–. (PL2)
"I'm uh, I'm uh, I'm going to marry Miss Machiko."

Mother: なに いってん の あんたは もー。
Nani itten no anta wa mo–.
"What are you talking about?" (PL2)

Man: 留ボー が お嫁さん かい、 ほっほっほっ。
Tomebō ga oyome-san kai ho! ho! ho!
"Tomebō is going to be a bride, is he? Ho! Ho! Ho!"

2nd Man: は は は はは。
"Ha ha ha ha ha!"

- *sensei* is frequently used as an honorific suffix with names (instead of *–san*), but using it with the teacher's first name has a kindergarten touch.
- *nani itten no* is a contraction of *nani o itte-(i)ru no*, a very informal (PL2) version of *nani o itte-imasu ka* ("What are you saying?").
- *kai* is a informal, friendly form of the question marker *ka*. *Kai* and *dai* (for *da*) are frequently used by children and by adults in speaking to children.

She is a little older than Tomebō (above), but she still uses her own name to refer to herself. Among female speakers, it's not uncommon for this practice to continue into the teen years. Her father loves to fish, and he always brings home such huge catches of *tai* (sea bream, considered quite a luxury/delicacy), that she is sick of it. In this scene she is saying how much she likes *rāmen*. This is something like an American child who has had too much steak, and would rather have a hot dog. The "Cooking Papa," Iwa-san, makes her some *tai rāmen*, and everyone is happy.

Momoko: ももこ ね、ラーメン だ〜い好き よっ!!
Momoko ne rāmen da–isuki yo!!
"I just lo-o-ove rāmen!!"

Iwa-san: そう か。
Sō ka.
"Is that so."

- the prefix *dai–* is sometimes written with the kanji for large/big (大), and *dai-suki* is used to express the idea "like very much" → "(just) love."

© Ueyama Tochi / *Cooking Papa*, Kōdansha

Adults using children's language

In our final two scenes we see adults talking to children in baby talk. In this scene from *Yawara*, Fujiko had quit jūdō to have her baby, but now she is beginning training again, intent on going to the Olympics. Her husband even helps out with the housework to encourage her to train.

© Urasawa Naoki / *Yawara!*, Shogakukan

Fujiko: お母さん、行ってきまちゅね〜 いい 子 で いて ね〜。
Okāsan,   itte kimachu   ne– ii   ko de ite   ne–.
mother   go and come back (colloq) good child as be (colloq)
"Mama is going out for a while. You be good, now."

Dad: いよいよ 始めます か!!
iyo iyo   hajimemasu ka!!
at last/finally start   (?)
"Are you about ready to start?!!"

- just as *desu* became *dechu* in an earlier example, *kimasu* becomes *kimachu* here. *Itte kimasu* is the standard expression used when going out for a while. It literally means "I will go and come (back)."
- *ii ko* means "good child," and *ite* (from the verb *iru*, "be") is short for *ite kudasai*, "Please be . . ." Dropping *kudasai* and using the *–te* form of a verb to make a request is pretty much the norm in informal speech.

The director is getting into it: Playing with his friend's daughter, he pretends to eat the imaginary food and uses baby talk. He carries the panda on his back like Japanese mothers carry their babies.

Man: はあ、おいちい。
Hā,   oichii.
"Ahh, it's yummy."

Momoko: は〜い、おかわりしましょう ね。
Ha–i,   okawarishimashō   ne.
"OK, let's give you seconds."

Sound FX: パク パク パク
Paku paku paku
(sound/effect of his pretending to eat)

- *okawari* is the honorific prefix *o–* with *kawari*, the noun form of the verb *kawaru* ("change/be replaced"). In this meaning of "another helping/serving of food or beverage" the *o–* is an integral part of the word.

© Ueyama Tochi / *Cooking Papa*, Kōdansha

バイバイ!!

Lesson 18 • Informal "Politeness"

As we always mention in the MANGAJIN warning about "Politeness Levels," the word "politeness" is really just a convenient simplification. There are actually several dimensions involved in "polite speech." For example, certain verbs are inherently honorific, and are used to show respect for, or deference toward, another person, but the endings of these verbs (which are a primary factor in the MANGAJIN system of "politeness levels"), are really more a function of the formality of the situation. This can lead to situations in which it's hard to know exactly which of MANGAJIN's four politeness levels is appropriate. In this lesson we look at a few such situations.

Our first three examples show informal usage of the verb *nasaru*, an honorific equivalent of the ordinary verb *suru*, meaning "do." Because it's honorific, *nasaru* is used only for the actions of others, never one's own actions. It indicates that you feel respect for the other person. When translating into English, it is almost impossible to make a distinction between *suru* and *nasaru* (except by using phrasing that might convey the tone somehow), but they are two different words that convey a very different feeling in Japanese.

Beginning students usually first encounter *nasaru* in its *–masu* form, *nasaimasu*. In MANGAJIN, *nasaimasu* is classified as PL4, the highest level. To convey the same meaning in what we call PL3, typically one would replace the honorific *nasaimasu* with *shimasu*, the PL3 form of *suru*. *Suru,* the plain abrupt form, is a clear case of PL2, but how do you rank *nasaru?* It still shows respect, and is clearly more "polite" than *suru*, so it wouldn't be right to call it PL2, but it's not really PL3 or PL4 either. Our manga examples illustrate this kind of dilemma in assigning politeness levels.

A traditional wife

Her husband has come home early so she knows something is wrong. Instead of the common PL2 expression *Dō shita no?*, she asks him *Dō nasatta no?*, substituting the honorific verb *nasaru* for the neutral verb *suru*. As you can see in the second frame where she is taking his coat, she shows the traditional respect for, or perhaps deference to, her husband. But they are husband and wife, and this is obviously an informal situation, so she uses the plain/abrupt past form, *nasatta*, instead of the more formal *nasaimashita*.

Observing the traditional social hierarchy in this way is considered a sign of good breeding or refinement. In fact, women's use of such "polite" words can often be more a matter of refinement than of respect — e.g., when they are speaking among themselves.

© Yamasaki & Kitami / *Tsuri-Baka Nisshi*, Shogakukan

Husband: ただいま。
Tadaima.
just now
"I'm home."

Wife: あら。 あなた、どうなさったの？
Ara.　　Anata,　dō nasatta no?
(exclam.) you/"dear"　what's wrong
"My goodness! What's wrong, Dear?"

Husband: ちょっと 風邪をひいた ようだ。
Chotto　　kaze o hiita　　yō da.
a little　　caught cold　　it seems that
"I seem to have caught a little cold."

Wife: そう ...
So ...
"Really?"

Feminine deference

A middle-aged salaryman, Nishimura-san, meets Natsuko, the daughter of a professor, at a mountain resort. Since they don't know each other very well, they both use primarily PL3 (–*masu/ desu*) speech, but because of the informal setting, some PL2 is mixed in too.

As a sign of feminine deference, she uses the honorific verb *nasaru* (*sukoshi mo nasaranai*) rather than the neutral verb *suru* (*sukoshi mo shinai*), but she uses the plain abrupt form *nasaranai* rather than the more formal *nasaimasen*.

© Saigan Ryōhei / *San-chōme no Yūhi,* Shogakukan

> **Natsuko:** だけど ご自分 の 話 は, 少しも なさらないのね。
> *Dakedo go-jibun no hanashi wa sukoshi mo nasaranai no ne*
> but (hon.) self of talk as-for even a little don't do (?) do you
> **"But you don't talk about yourself at all, do you?"**

- *sukoshi mo* followed by a negative verb means that the action (talking) occurs "not even a little/ not at all."

Deference/respect for royalty

The young king has developed a tumor on his forehead and is in such intense pain that he cannot eat, sleep, or even lie still. The court physician, Jiiwaka, suggests removing it surgically, but Buddha relieves the pain with the touch of his finger. As an older, respected member of the court, Jiiwaka uses mostly informal speech forms, but as a sign of respect for the king, he uses the honorific verb *nasaru* (*jitto nasatte-ru*) instead of the neutral verb *suru* (*jitto shite-ru*).

© Tezuka Osamu / *Buddha,* Tezuka Productions

> **Jiiwaka:** 信じられん。 陛下 が 心地よさそうに 目 を つむられてじっとなさってる。
> *Shinjiraren. Heika ga kokochi yosasō ni me o tsumurarete jitto nasatte-ru.*
> can't believe His Majesty (subj.) appears to be comfortably eyes (obj.) closed-and is being still (hon.)
> **"I can't believe it . . . His Majesty appears comfortable, lying still with his eyes shut. "**

- *shinjiraren* is an informal masculine form of *shinjirarenai* ("cannot believe"), the plain negative form of *shinjirareru* ("can believe"), from the verb *shinjiru* ("believe").
- *kokochi yoi* means "comfortable/pleasant," and *kokochi yosasō* is used to indicate that someone else appears to be comfortable.
- *tsumurarete* is also honorific — an honorific –*te* form of *tsumuru*, "close (one's) eyes." This is identical to the passive form of the verb.

The "polite" verb *itadaku*: students generally encounter this word first as *itadakimasu*, the "thanks" said before partaking of a meal or beverage. It means "receive/partake of/have done on one's behalf," but it's a humble word, implying that the receiver/partaker is of a lower or subordinate status. The verb *morau* has the same meaning, but implies that both parties are equal, or that the receiver is of higher status. In the following two examples, women are shown using *itadaku* in a way which, although certainly not limited to females, gives an air of refinement to feminine speech.

Feminine and refined, but informal

Buying a watch: this woman is the customer, so social hierarchy certainly does not dictate that she use polite/humble speech. Her use of the humble word *itadaku* (instead of the neutral word *morau*) gives an air of refinement, but she uses the informal form, *itadaku*, instead of the more formal *itadakimasu*. The honorific *o-* before *ikura* also adds to the air of refinement.

© Takeda & Takai / *Pro Golfer*, Shogakukan

Woman: そう... 　　いい 　　感じ 　　ね。
Sō 　　*ii* 　　*kanji* 　　*ne.*
that's so/really 　good 　feel/effect/impression 　(colloq.)
"Really . . . It seems nice."

いただく 　　　　わ。 　　おいくら？
Itadaku 　　　　*wa.* 　　*o-ikura?*
(I'll) receive/take (it) 　(fem.) 　(hon.) how much
"I'll take it. How much?"

• her initial *sō* ("That's so") is in response to the clerk's explanation about the merits of this watch, i.e. she is agreeing that it is light and has a nice design.

From *Urusei Yatsura*: Oyuki, the princess of Neptune, traveled through a fourth dimensional passageway to the room of "ordinary" high school student Ataru. She is leaving now and asks if someone won't escort her back. As a princess among ordinary humans, she is free to use whatever speech forms she likes, but using the humble word *itadakenai* (*okutte itadakenai*) instead of the neutral *moraenai* (*okutte moraenai*) gives a feminine, refined touch. Because of the informal setting and the social status of the others present, however, she uses *itadakenai* instead of the more formal *itadakemasen*.

© Takahashi Rumiko / *Urusei Yatsura*, Shogakukan

Oyuki: 送って いただけない 　　　　かしら！
Okutte itadakenai 　　　　*kashira!*
can't have (someone) take/escort (me) (I) wonder
"I wonder if I couldn't have someone accompany me!"

Ataru: ハイッ！
Hai!
sure/all right
"Sure!"

• *itadakenai* is the plain/abrupt negative of *itadakeru* ("can receive/can have done"), which is the potential form of *itadaku* ("receive/have done").

Chivalrous? use of polite speech

At a pro golf tournament, her hat was blown off by a strong gust of wind just as he was making a shot. The ball goes in the hat, which, carried by the wind, deposits the ball right on the green. He returns the hat to her, and she apologizes for interfering with his game. He reassures her, and then takes the opportunity to ask for her phone number.

As you might guess from the golf tee that he carries in his mouth, Typhoon is a laid-back type who generally uses informal (PL2) speech. Here, he first says *tasukete moratta*, and he could have said *Denwa bangō o oshiete moraitai*, but by ending with a more "polite" or honorific word in its plain form, he implies that he is a gentleman while maintaining his casual identity.

© Takahashi & Kazama / *Dr. Taifūn JR*, Futabasha

Dr. Typhoon: いや ワタシの 方 こそ あなたに たすけて もらった のだ。
Iya watashi no hō koso anata ni tasukete moratta no da.
no　my　side (emph.)　you　by　received saving/help　(emph.)
"No, I'm the one who was helped by you."

ぜひ　電話番号　を　教えていただきたい。
Zehi denwa bangō o oshiete itadakitai.
definitely　phone number　(obj.)　want to receive your telling
"I definitely would like to have you tell me your phone number."
→ **"Won't you please tell me your phone number?"**

Woman: でも ...
Demo ...
"But ..."

For more information

敬語 ***keigo*, "polite speech,"** is undeniably one of the most difficult aspects of becoming fully proficient in Japanese. It's nice to know that you are "safe" in most situations if you stick to the PL3 *desu/-masu* endings — you're unlikely to offend anyone too badly — but you can never aspire to "natural" Japanese unless you are ready to tackle polite speech. This is the area where language and culture become almost inseparable. For those who are ready to push their politeness skills to a new level, here are some recent books that should help.

- *Minimum Essential Politeness: A Guide to the Japanese Honorific Language*, by Agnes M. Niyekawa (Kodansha International, 1991). This is a practical book, offering not only a clear explanation of all the factors that must be considered to establish the appropriate level of politeness but also presenting handy charts of the most important words and forms and step-by-step guides for learning the complex system (what to learn first in order to avoid the worst rudeness; what to learn next to refine your politeness).

- *How to Be Polite in Japanese*, by Osamu Mizutani and Nobuko Mizutani (The Japan Times, 1987), is similar in offering an analysis of the system and charts of the most important words and forms. It also discusses such practical matters as what *not* to talk about, non-verbal expressions of politeness, and a number of specific interactive situations.

- *Formal Expressions for Japanese Interaction*, edited by staff of the Inter-University Center for Japanese Language Studies (The Japan Times, 1991). This is an exercise-filled textbook, with accompanying tapes, rather than a systematic presentation of honorific speech as such. From one lesson to the next, foreign student David Smith interacts with Japanese of widely varied ages and status. The exercises give students practice not only in honorific forms but in other aspects of usage, such as indirect speech, that affect politeness. This one is designed to be used with a teacher.

Lesson 19 • Introductions

Most textbooks give "formula" introductions which are perfectly acceptable and quite helpful to beginners, but as you will see from the examples we present in this lesson, "real" introductions use an almost random mix of a few basic elements.

Introducing the introduction

The word for "introduction" in Japanese is *shōkai* (紹介), and its verb form is *shōkai suru*, or, at PL3, *shōkai shimasu*. It's quite common for people to begin introductions by using some form of *shōkai suru,* which literally means "I will introduce . . .," but functions like the English, "I'd like to introduce . . .," or "Let me introduce . . ."

Giving names

The simplest way to introduce yourself is to say your name followed by *desu*, making a sentence equivalent to English "I am So-and-so." Gesture toward your friend and say his/her name followed by *desu*, and it becomes "This is So-and-so."

A more formal way to introduce someone else is *Kochira wa . . . desu. Kochira* is literally "this side/direction," but it means "the person here/in this direction." In other contexts, "this" is translated as *kore*, and *Kore wa . . . desu* is sometimes used to make an introduction, but only in very informal situations, and mostly by males. You need to be careful because some people will be offended at being treated like a "thing" if you refer to them as *kore*.

Another way to give your own name is with the expressions *. . . to ii masu* (といいます) or *. . . to mōshimasu* (と申します). Saying your name followed by *to iimasu* is literally "I'm called (name)," and could be compared to saying "My name is . . ." in English. The expression *. . . to mōshimasu* is a PL4 humble expression that means the same thing, but is used when the situation is formal or calls for a higher level of politeness.

Greetings

In addition to the name/basic information, some kind of greeting is usually part of the introduction routine.

Hajimemashite (初めまして)
This literally means "[I meet you] for the first time" but for some reason, most textbooks "translate" it as "How do you do?"

Yoroshiku o-negai shimasu (よろしくお願いします)
This phrase literally means "I ask you to treat me favorably/I ask your favorable consideration," and its use is not limited to introductions. It doesn't really have an equivalent in English, but in introductions it's generally "translated" as "I'm pleased to meet you."

Kochira koso (こちらこそ)
This isn't a greeting in itself, but rather a response to the other person's *Yoroshiku . . .* Since *kochira* means "this side/direction" and *koso* is an emphasizer meaning "indeed/even more so," in essence the phrase means "Even more than you, I must ask *your* favorable consideration."

Dōmo (どうも)
This word is really only an emphasizer, meaning "indeed/really/quite," but as we noted in Lesson 8, it has become a kind of "all–purpose word" that can fill in for much more complicated greetings and expressions, or simply to avoid having to figure out what the appropriate thing to say in a given situation is.

Bow

Don't forget the bow if it's a formal introduction, or a friendly nod if it's very informal!

Mix and match: As you can see in our examples, the exchange in an introduction can range from complex to very simple. If you know the basic elements and adjust them to an appropriate politeness level, you can introduce and be introduced with the best of them.

The rookie and the old pro

Their relative status is reflected in their speech and posture. Wakatabe, a young rookie, is introducing himself to Kageura, a 45-year-old veteran of 20 seasons of professional baseball. In deference to Kageura's seniority, Wakatabe uses polite (PL3) speech, while Kageura responds with plain (PL2) speech. This difference in speech is also reflected in their posture — Wakatabe is striking a somewhat formal pose (hands at sides, bowing slightly), while Kageura is more relaxed and informal. They have both removed their caps for this exchange.

Kageura, the hero of this series, is a fictional character, but Wakatabe Ken'ichi is a real baseball player with the Daiei Hawks. Having real athletes appear alongside fictional characters is not unusual in sports manga.

Wakatabe: あ、あのー、 若田部健一 です。 よろしく おねがいします。
A, ano– Wakatabe Ken'ichi desu. Yoroshiku onegaishimasu.
"U, uhh, I'm Wakatabe Ken'ichi. I'm pleased to meet you." (PL3)

Kageura: 景浦 だ。 こちら こそ よろしく。
Kageura da. Kochira koso yoroshiku.
"I'm Kageura. My pleasure." (PL2)

Sound FX: ザワァ ザワァァ
Zawā zawā—
(the buzz of the crowd; also used as a rustling sound)

カシャ カシャ カシャ カシャ カシャ
Kasha kasha kasha kasha kasha
(soft clicking of camera shutters)

ジー
Jii
(whirring sound of camcorder)

I'm called . . . (humble)

The man on the right is a new employee, so he uses the humble . . . *to mōshimasu* when introducing himself. The company is a small finance company with a fairly high level of employee turnover, and so the hierarchy is not as clearly defined as in a large corporation. Both these men are about the same age, and in this informal setting, the new employee, Yoshimura, abbreviates the second part of his self-introduction from *Yoroshiku o-negai shimasu* to a simple *Yoroshiku*.

© Aoki Yūji / *Naniwa Kinyū-do*, Kōdansha

Yoshimura: 吉村　　と 申します。よろしく。
Yoshimura to mōshimasu. Yoroshiku.
<u>**"My name is Yoshimura. Pleased to meet you."**</u>
(PL4-2)

Haibara: こちら こそ。　灰原 です。
Kochira koso. Haibara desu.
<u>**"My pleasure. I'm Haibara."**</u> (PL3)

I'm called . . . (neutral)

In the same office as the example above, a senior employee introduces himself to the new employee, Yoshimura.

© Aoki Yūji / *Naniwa Kinyū-do*, Kōdansha

Motoki: どうも。ワシ 元木 と いいます。よろしく。
Dōmo. Washi Motoki to iimasu. Yoroshiku.
<u>**Hi. My name is Motoki. Pleased to meet you."**</u> (PL3-2)

Yoshimura: こちら　こそ よろしくお願いします。
Kochira koso yoroshiku onegaishimasu.
<u>**"The pleasure is all mine."**</u> (PL3)

• *dōmo* sometimes serves as a kind of verbal warm-up, rather than a short form of any particular greeting.
• *washi* is a variation of *watashi* ("I/me") used by older men.

Hajimemashite in a standard introduction

This woman runs a *bentō* (box lunch) business, and needs some help with a big order. Her friend, Akane-san, has come to help out. In this scene she is introducing Akane-san to her mother-in-law.

© Nagamatsu Kiyoshi / *Torao-san no O-ki ni Iri*, Kōdansha

1st Woman: お義母さん　紹介します。　　こちら　　今日　　1日　　手伝ってくれる　三ノ宮あかねさん。
Okāsan　　　shōkai shimasu.　Kochira　kyō　ichinichi　tetsudatte kureru　Sannomiya Akane-san.
mother-in-law　will introduce　this direction　today　one day　will help me/us　(name-hon.)
"Mother, let me introduce (my friend). This is Sannomiya Akane, who is helping me out today."
(PL3)

Sannomiya: 初めまして。　　三ノ宮　あかね です。
Hajimemashite. Sannomiya Akane　desu.
"How do you do. I'm Sannomiya Akane." (PL3)

Hajimemashite in a variation

From the popular series *Kachō Shima Kōsaku*, Shima has been instructed by his boss to check up on a certain bar hostess. His boss has told the "mama" of the bar about Shima, but they have never met. In this first panel, the "mama" greets Shima as she would any new customer. Shima chooses to let his *meishi* (名刺, "business card") do the talking.

Mama: いらっしゃいませ。初めまして。
Irasshaimase.　　　Hajimemashite.
"Welcome. How do you do." (PL3)

Narration: ママ　が　来た！
Mama ga kita!
"The 'mama' came!" (PL3)

Shima: や、どうも。　私　はこういう者　でして...
Ya, dōmo. Watashi wa kō iu mono deshite...
"Uh, hello. I'm this kind of person."
→ **"Uh, hello. Let me give you my card."** (PL3)

© Hirokane Kenshi / *Kachō Shima Kōsaku*, Kōdansha

Getting informal

The boss, a *kachō* in this case, has invited one of his employees and the "mama-san" of his favorite bar to go fishing with him. In making the introduction, he does not give her name, only her "title." Both men are likely to continue to refer to her as "mama-san."

© Yamasaki & Kitami / *Tsuri-Baka Nisshi*, Shogakukan

Boss: こちら　銀座　"ミミ"　の　ママさん。
Kochira Ginza "Mimi" no mama-san.
<u>**"This is the 'mama-san' of Ginza (club) Mimi."**</u> (PL2)

Female friend: よろしく　ネ。
Yoroshiku ne.
<u>**"Pleased to meet you."**</u> (PL2)

Employee: はあ...
Hā...
<u>**"Aah..."**</u>

An informal & abrupt introduction

High school students, especially males, tend to use abrupt forms. Using *kore* ("this [one/thing]") instead of *kochira* would be impolite in most situations. He also omits the particle *wa* after *kore*, and drops the verb at the end.

© Saigan Ryōhei / *San-chōme no Yūhi*, Shogakukan

Boy: あ、これ　友達　の　熊谷。
A, Kore tomodachi no Kumatani.
"Ah, this is my friend, Kumatani." (PL2)

Kumatani: よ、よろしく。
Yo- yoroshiku.
"Ple–, pleased to meet you." (PL2)

Runner: こんちは、兄貴　がお世語　になってます!
Konchi wa. Aniki ga o-sewa ni natte-masu!
"Hello. Thanks for looking out for my big brother!" (PL3)

- 熊谷 is usually read *Kumagai*, but earlier in the story his name is given as *Kumatani*.
- *aniki* is an informal word for "big brother."
- *sewa* (世話) means "help/aid/good offices," and *sewa ni natte-(i)masu* means that someone is being helped or is benefiting from a person's good offices. In this case, the boys are just friends, so it's simply a platitude.

Complicated introduction, simple response

A third party (off-panel) is introducing these two and giving a little background on each. The introduction might be a little complicated, but their responses are simplicity itself. It's difficult to determine the sequence of their lines. In this case, he is probably responding *Dōmo* to her *Hajimemashite* even as he is being introduced, but the sequence could just as easily be reversed.

© Ueyama Tochi / *Cooking Papa*, Kōdansha

> **Introducer:** こいつ は オレの　幼なじみ　で達っちゃん。
> *Koitsu wa ore no osana-najimi de Tat-chan.*
> **"This guy is my childhood friend, Tatchan."** (PL2)

> **Woman:** はじめましてー。
> *Hajimemashite–.*
> **"How do you do."** (PL3)

> **Introducer:** で こちら うち の 総務課 のやりて主任　池田 敏子女史。
> *De kochira uchi no sōmu-ka no yarite shunin, Ikeda Toshiko-joshi.*
> **"And this is the go-getter manager from our general affairs section, Miss Ikeda Toshiko."** (PL2-3)

> **Man:** あっ、どーもどーも。
> *A! dōmo dōmo.*
> **"Ah! Really, really."** (PL3)

• unable to come up with any kind of inspired translation for *dōmo*, we went with a literal rendering. By using *dōmo*, he avoids having to choose a specific greeting and politeness level.

The essence of simplicity

Hiroko and Kōsuke, the couple on the left, are girlfriend and boyfriend. They have stopped in a shop where one of Hiroko's friends works.

> **Friend:** 彼氏?
> *Kareshi?*
> **"(Your) boyfriend?"**

> **Hiroko:** 耕助くん。
> **"Kōsuke-kun."**

> **Kōsuke:** ども。
> *Domo.*
> **"Hi."**

© Maekawa Tsukasa / *Dai-Tōkyō Binbō Seikatsu Manyuaru*, Kōdansha

Lesson 20 • "-*sama*" words

The -*sama* ending is usually first encountered as a more polite form of -*san*, the suffix for names that's essentially equivalent to the titles "Mr./Ms./Mrs." in English. It is also used to make family terms like *okāsan* ("mother") and *otōsan* ("father") more polite, as when referring to someone else's family members or when you need to address members of your own family in a particularly polite manner: *okāsama, otōsama*.

The -*sama* words we show you in this lesson are also polite expressions, but they have nothing to do with names or family. *Gokurō-sama*, for example, is the word *kurō* (苦労), meaning "trouble/suffering/hard work," with the honorific prefix *go-* and the honorific ending -*sama*, but it doesn't mean "The Honorable Mr. Trouble." It means "Thank you for your trouble/hard work."

The other words we illustrate here all follow the same pattern of a word framed by an honorific prefix (*o-* or *go-*) and the honorific ending -*sama*. None can be translated literally, but most of the ones we've chosen are used in situations where an English speaker would say "Thank you for . . . ," or perhaps simply "Thank you." Two of the examples can be thought of as apologies.

Adding *desu* or *deshita*, according to the situation, makes the expression sound more formal. In informal situations most -*sama* words can be changed to -*san*, or the -*sama*/-*san* ending can be dropped altogether — though this is not necessarily true of all -*sama* words. Even when the ending is dropped altogether, though, the honorific prefix (*o-* or *go-*) must be kept. *Gokurō-sama* reduced to *gokurō* still means "Thank you for your trouble/hard work," but without the prefix *go-* it becomes just an ordinary noun meaning "trouble/suffering/hard work."

We begin with several examples of *gokurō-sama* and the quite similar *otsukare-sama*. Then we present four other frequently used -*sama* words.

Accepting a delivery

Her family in the country has sent her a box of potatoes, and as the delivery man brings the heavy load into her front hall, she thanks him for his labors by saying *gokurō-sama*.

© Kobayashi Makoto / *What's Michael?*, Kodansha

Delivery Man: 印鑑 おねがいしま〜〜す!!
Inkan　o-negai shima–su!!
seal　　　please
"**I need you to sign for this!!**" (PL3)

Housewife: どうも、ごくろうさま〜〜。
Dōmo,　gokurō-sama–.
"**Thank you so much (for your trouble).**" (PL2)

• *inkan* (also referred to as *hanko*) is the small seal most adult Japanese carry with them for use in situations where Americans would be required to give a signature.

Thanking in advance

The woman on the left is visiting her husband in the hospital. The nurse has come to take the patient's blood pressure.

© Sakata & Kazama / *Kaze no Daichi,* Shogakukan

Nurse: 血圧 を はかります。
Ketsuatsu o hakarimasu.
blood pressure (obj.) will measure
"I'll take his blood pressure." (PL3)

Patient's wife: あ、 ごくろうさまです。
A, gokurō-sama desu.
"Thank you (for your trouble)." (PL3)

Thanking after the fact

An informant has brought a tape recording of police discussions about a critical case. The *kurō* (of making the tape and smuggling it out of the building) was performed earlier, so the past form, *Gokurō-sama deshita,* is appropriate.

© Saitō Takao / *Gorugo 13 Series,* Shogakukan

Mr. Chachai: ご苦労様 でした。
Gokurō-sama deshita.
"Thank you for your troubles." (PL3)

これ は お約束の お礼 です。
Kore wa o-yakusoku no o-rei desu.
this as-for (hon.)-promised (hon.)-fee is
"This is the fee/reward we promised you." (PL3)

Informant: どうも。
Dōmo.
"Thanks." (PL3)

- (*o-*)*rei* can mean "gratitude/thanks," but it is typically used to refer to fees paid to certain professionals.
- *dōmo* is really only an emphasizer, meaning "indeed/really/very much," but here it is shorthand for *dōmo arigatō gozaimasu,* "thank you very much."

An informal version—*gokurō-san*

He is thanking the cats for warming up the futon. Just as *-san* is less formal than *-sama* when used with a name, *gokurō-san* is less formal than *gokurō-sama*. As you can tell from his expression, there's a touch of sarcasm here.

Man: よ〜〜し, ごくろうさん。
Yo–shi,　　gokurō-san.
"All right, thanks for your trouble." (PL2-3)

© Kobayashi Makoto / *What's Michael?*, Kodansha

An overlap of *gokurō-sama* and *otsukare-sama*

***Otsukare-sama* comes from** the verb *tsukareru*, "become/grow tired," so the expression essentially thanks the listener for efforts that are presumed to have tired him out. That makes its basic meaning very similar to *gokurō-sama,* and in this example, where two women thank the hotel staff for their efforts when the hotel bus became stuck in a snowstorm, both expressions can be used. The two are not fully interchangeable, though. It's generally best to avoid using *gokurō-sama* with persons of higher status, but this restriction does not apply for *otsukare-sama (deshita)*.

© Ishinomori Shōtarō / *Hotel*, Shogakukan

1st Woman: お疲れさま　でした。
Otsukare-sama deshita.
"It must have been a tiring experience." (PL3)

2nd Woman: 本当　に ご苦労さま　でした ね。
Hontō ni gokurō-sama deshita　ne.
"Thank you very much for all your efforts." (PL3)

The hard-working writer

The man in the bottom frame works for a magazine publisher and is picking up a manuscript from the writer in the top frame.

© Saigan Ryōhei / *San-chōme no Yūhi*, Shogakukan

Kitano: どうも お疲れさま でした、先生。
Dōmo otsukare-sama deshita, sensei.
"Thank you for your tireless efforts, Mr. Yamao." (PL3)

また 来月号 も、よろしく お願いします。
Mata raigetsu-gō mo, yoroshiku o-negai shimasu.
again next month's issue also favorably please
"I hope we can count on you for next month's issue, as well." (PL3)

- in addition to the meaning "teacher," *sensei* is also used as a title of respect for various professionals, especially if they have achieved prominence in their field. Depending on the profession involved, it can mean "Doctor (medical or otherwise)," "Professor," etc. Since this is a writer, we went with a simple "Mr."

Three variations

After a long video shoot, the model and the crew exchange *otsukare*s in varying levels of formality. Although the model may be making more money than the crew members, she uses the most polite speech form partly because she is young and female.

© Yajima & Hirokane / *Ningen Kōsaten*, Shogakukan

Crew 1: お疲れさん。
Otsukare-san.
"Thank you." (PL3)

Crew 2: お疲れ!
Otsukare!
"Thanks!" (PL3-2)

Model: お疲れさま でした!
Otsukare-sama deshita!
"Thank you very much!" (PL3)

- these variations of "Thank you" don't really correspond to the varying politeness levels of *otsukare*. In fact, the PL labels we have assigned are rather arbitrary.

Omachidō-sama

The standard line used by waiters and waitresses when serving a customer is *Omachidō-sama (deshita)*. *Machidō* is from the adjective *machidōi* or *machidōshii*, which refers to waiting impatiently for something that is long in coming, and *omachidō-sama* can be thought of as meaning either "Thank you for waiting" or "Sorry to have kept you waiting."

© Nakajima Tōru / *Puro no Hitori Goto*, Shogakukan

Waiter: おまちどーさまーー。
Omachido-sama—.
"Sorry to have kept you waiting." (PL3-2)

Customer: うむ。
Umu.
"Mmm." (PL2)

Osewa-sama

Leaving the doctor's office, this child's mother uses the expression *osewa-sama*. *Sewa* (世話) means "help/aid/good offices," so *osewa-sama* means "Thank you for your help." The child has been something of a terror during the visit — hence the doctor's concern about his blood pressure.

© Usui Yoshihito / *Kureyon Shin-chan*, Futabasha

Mother: ど、どうも お世話様 でした。
Do, dōmo osewa-sama deshita.
"Thank you for your help." (PL3)

Child: 元気 だして ね。
Genki dashite ne.
"Chin up, now." (PL2)

Sound FX: はあ はあ はあ
Hā hā hā
(sound of heavy breathing)

Doctor: け、血圧 が...
Ke, ketsuatsu ga...
"M- my blood pressure..."

Nurse: せ、先生...
Se, sensei...
"D-doctor..."

Gochisō-sama

In a restaurant or at home, *gochisō-sama* is the appropriate way to thank the one who prepared/provided the meal. The expression can be used to thank someone for any gift of food.

© Abe & Kurata / *Aji Ichimon Me,* Shogakukan

Sound FX: ワイ　ワイ
Wai　wai
(boisterous noise of diners)

ハハハ　　ハハハ
Ha ha ha　Ha ha ha
(laughing)

Woman: ごちそうさま　でした。
Gochisō-sama　deshita.
"Thank you (for a wonderful meal)." (PL3)

Osomatsu-sama

At a karaoke bar, this woman is apologizing for her poor singing with an expression that comes from *somatsu* ("coarse/crude/inferior/shabby"). She is likely to apologize this way even if she sang very well — as a matter of modesty. Using this same expression, a modest host or hostess will respond to a guest's *gochisō-sama* with an apology implying the food was coarse/inadequate/poorly prepared no matter how sumptuous the feast may have been.

© Nōjō Jun'ichi / *Prince,* Shogakukan

1st Woman: うまい!!
Umai!!

サイコー!!
Saikō!!

アンコール!!
Ankōru!!
"Good!! Great!! Encore!!"
(PL2)

Sound FX: パチッ　パチッ　パチッ
Pachi　pachi　pachi
(clapping sound)

2nd Woman: おそまつさま　でした!!
Osomatsu-sama　deshita!!
"It was awful!!" (PL3)

Lesson 21 • Hesitating with *anō . . .*

Anō*, or its short form *ano, is a word — or you might say it's just a "sound" — that expresses a feeling of hesitation. For example, when you're hesitating over what to say next, *anō* can fill the pause, just like "uh" in English. Learning to say *anō* instead of "uh" when you are struggling to remember the Japanese word for something will go a long way toward making your Japanese sound more natural, though, as with "uh," one must be careful not to overdo it.

Anō can also be used to get the attention of someone you wish to speak to, something like the way "excuse me" is used in English when approaching someone to ask a question or otherwise interrupt what they are doing. In such situations, *anō* expresses the speaker's hesitation to bother the listener, thereby showing consideration for the listener. So, regardless of the politeness level of the rest of what is said, *anō* in this usage has a certain quality of politeness (though it can't be assigned to any particular politeness level). Since "polite" is not a word we would associate with "uh" in English, it's important to think of this use of *anō* as overlapping with that of "excuse me."

The word is used to show other kinds of hesitation in the course of a conversation as well, such as when one wishes to contradict/reject what the other person has said *(anō, sore wa chotto . . .* — "Excuse me but that's a little [mistaken/disagreeable/unacceptable]"); when one is about to break some bad news *(anō, chotto iizurai n desu ga . . .* — "Uh, it's a little hard for me/I'm sorry to have to say this, but . . ."); or, when one is worried about sounding too forward. These uses, too, have a certain feeling of politeness because by expressing hesitation, they show the speaker's consideration for the listener's feelings.

In some cases *anō* is used without any feeling of polite hesitation or of struggling to find the right words; instead it simply signals that the speaker is starting to say something and wants the listener's particular attention, similar to English use of words like "look/say/now/well" at the beginning of statements. We have sometimes described this as a kind of "verbal warm-up/tee-up" in our manga notes. It's often a hard line to draw, though, since the other uses of *anō* can also be thought of as "warm-ups" for what follows.

Anō as "Excuse me"

The high school was in Shikoku, but this is a meeting of classmates who are now living in Tokyo. This young man was reluctant to come because he is pursuing a career as an *enka* singer and has not achieved any kind of financial success. In addition, he still has a rural accent which he has recently become acutely aware of. As he timidly opens the door, he says *ano* to get the receptionist's attention — a situation where an English speaker might say "Excuse me."

© Tsuchida Saiki / *Orebushi,* Shogakukan

Kōji: あ . . . あの . . .
A . . . ano . . .
"<u>Uh . . . Excuse me . . .</u>"

Receptionist: あっ、 ハイハイ 受け付け ね!
A! Hai hai, uketsuke ne!
"Oh, yes, yes, registration, right?" (PL2)

* *uketsuke* can refer to a "receptionist/reception desk" or to the act of "checking in/registering" for an event.

When interrupting another conversation

This man and woman used to date each other, but in this scene she is having dinner with another man (her boss, it turns out). He interrupts their conversation to ask to speak to her.

© Tsukamoto Tomoko / *Karā-na Ai,* Shogakukan

<u>Kurimoto:</u> あの、ちょっと 話がしたい ん だけど。
Ano, chotto hanashi ga shitai n dakedo.
uhh, a little want to talk (explan) it is, but
"Excuse me, I'd like to have a word with you."

At a delicate time

She has just found out that she is pregnant, and she is about to confide in her (young, attractive) supervisor. Their conversation is overheard, and everyone in the office thinks they are having an affair.

© Hijiri Hideo / *Dakara Shōsuke,* Shogakukan

<u>Shōsuke:</u> やあ 中島クン。
Yā Nakajima-kun.
Hey Nakajima
"Yo, Nakajima." (PL3)

- *kun* is typically used with the names of young males, but it can also be used with OLs by their superiors.

<u>Secretary:</u> あのう、ちょっと いいですか、 笑介係長!?
Anō, chotto ii desu ka, Shōsuke-kakarichō?
uhh, a little is it OK (name) group chief
"Excuse me, can I speak to you just a minute, Shōsuke?" (PL3)

- *kakarichō* is a rank below *kachō* (section chief). *Kakari* refers to being "in charge" of a certain job/task and can apply either to an individual or a group. The suffix *-chō* indicates the chief/head of a group.

Trying not to sound too forward

She meets an older man and they enjoy each other's company, but as he is leaving, she realizes she never found out his name. Afraid of sounding too forward, she only implies the question (uses an abbreviated form), and warms up with *anō*.

Kuroishi: あ、あのぉ...ごめんなさい、
A, anō . . .　　　gomen-nasai,
U, uh . . .　　　　I'm sorry
"U-Uh, excuse me,

アタシ　　お名前を...
Atashi　　o-namae o . . .
I　　　　your name (obj)
"I (didn't get) your name."

© Iwashige Takashi / *Zappera*, Shogakukan

Later that evening

She gets a call from the man she met that day. This *ano* is probably both an expression of the man's hesitation/nervousness over making what might be construed as an over-eager call and a pause-filler while he fumbles for how to begin the conversation.

© Iwashige Takashi / *Zappera*, Shogakukan

Suzuki: ああの... 今日、お会いした 鈴木 です。
A-ano . . .　Kyō,　o-ai shita　Suzuki　desu.
U-uhh . . .　today　met　(name)　am
"I am Suzuki who met you today."
→ **"U-uhh . . . this is Suzuki — I met you today."** (PL3)

Kuroishi: 鈴木さん!?
"Suzuki-san!?"

• *o-ai shita* is a polite/humble past form of *au* ("meet"), here modifying the name Suzuki → "Suzuki, who met you."

Reluctant to say it

The young man in this scene is trying to find a girl he met only once at a bookstore. It's not clear if he really has the wrong party, or if the girl at the other end of the line is just pretending to be someone else. In either case, her *ano* expresses her hesitation at saying what she has to say, and serves to take the edge off of a response that could be painful to her listener.

© Iwashige Takashi / *Banei Kakeru*, Shogakukan

Voice: あの...言ってる こと が よく わからない。
Ano ... Itte-ru koto ga yoku wakaranai.
Uhh saying thing/fact (subj) well isn't understood
"Uhh ... I don't understand very well what you are saying."
→ **"I'm sorry ... I don't really know what you're talking about."** (PL3)

Ano as a "tee-up"

In the first panel, she is a little unsure and stutters her *ano*, but in the second frame she is smiling and her hesitation is apparently gone, so the *ano* can be thought of simply as a verbal "tee up" for the rest of the sentence.

© Tsukamoto Tomoko / *Karā-na Ai*, Shogakukan

Takada:
じゃ また。
Ja mata.
then/well again
"Then, see you later."

Sakaguchi: あ、あの...
A, ano ...
"Oh, uhh ..."

Sakaguchi: あの、 よかったら お茶 ご一緒 しませんか?
Ano, yokattara ocha go-issho shimasen ka?
Uhh/say if you'd like tea (hon) together won't you do/have
"Say, if you'd like, won't you have tea with us?"

133

Searching for the right words

From *Garcia-kun,* a manga about Hispanic *gaijin* in Japan, this panel shows one of Garcia's friends trying to find the right words to say to a bank teller. Actually, he has fallen in love and is about to propose to her right in the bank. If we assume he speaks first, then his *ano* also contains an element of "excuse me," for getting her attention, but in this context it is clearly the lesser element.

Customer: あの . . .
Ano . . .
"Uhh . . ."

Teller: いらっしゃいませ。
Irasshaimase.
"Welcome." → **"Yes sir."** (PL4)

Signs: 預金   スーパーMMC
Yokin   *Sūpā MMC*
Savings   **Super MMC**

- MMC stands for "Money Market Certificate." The minimum for a MMC used to be around ¥20 million, but the "Super MMC" can be used with smaller amounts.

© Takeuchi Akira / *Garushia-kun,* Futabasha

Later at the reunion . . .

Still embarrassed by his appearance and his dialect, the young man in our first illustration is unsure how to respond to this attractive former classmate (who has something of a crush on him).

Midori: トナリ   いーい?
Tonari   *i–i?*
next to/adjacent OK
"Can I sit next to you?" (PL2)

- this is a very abbreviated, colloquial style of speaking. Adding a simple *desu ka* on the end would make it more conventional, and would probably sound more natural for a beginning speaker of Japanese.

Kōji: あ . . . あの . . . ハイ . . .
A . . . ano . . . hai . . .
"U . . . Uhh . . . yes . . ." (PL3)

Midori: どう?   / その後 . . .   歌ってる?
Dō?   / *Sono go . . .*   *utatte-ru?*
How is it?   / after that   singing
"How's it going? Still singing?" (PL2)

Kōji: あ . . . あの . . . ハイ . . .
A . . . ano . . . hai . . .
"U . . . Uhh . . . yes . . ." (PL3)

- *sono go . . . utatte-ru?* is a very shorthand way of saying something like "Have you done any singing since then (the last time I saw you)?"

© Tsuchida Saiki / *Orebushi,* Shogakukan

When *anō* isn't enough to fill the pause

This outspoken daughter of the Arashiyama family (notorious for its constant squabbling and open discord) is coercing Yamano-san to admit that his family, in spite of its outward appearance of harmony and peacefulness, has just as many problems. Akira is usually a male name, but given her aggressive attitude and unladylike behavior, it seems appropriate for her.

© Wakabayashi Kenji / *Heisei Arashiyama Ikka*, Shogakukan

Akira:
ほら、言ってやんなさい よ、ズバッと!!
Hora,   itte yan-nasai   yo, zuba-tto!!
(exclam)   say (command) (emph) decisively
"Look, come on out and say it!!"

- *yan-nasai* is a contraction of *yari-nasai*, a command form of *yaru* ("give/do for"). *Itte yaru* means "say/tell to" someone else — in this case, to a third party.

Yamano: あっ... あの...
A!...   ano...
"Uh ... Uhh..." (PL2)

Yamano: え...えとー、 / いや...だから...
E...etō, / iya...dakara...
"Er ... Well ... I mean ... That is to say ..."

Try to avoid this situation

If you lose your passport, here's how to tell someone in Japanese. Although it's unlikely you'll have to ask someone to reissue your passport in Japanese, the same phrase will work if you lose your *gaijin tōroku-sho*, i.e. alien registration! The initial *ano* is optional, but it's a natural way to start a statement like this.

© Isshiki & Yamamoto / *Bokura wa Minna Ikite-iru*, Shogakukan

Takahashi: あの... パスポート 紛失して、
Ano...   pasupōto   funshitsu shite,
Uhh...   passport   lost (and)
再発行してほしい んだ けど...
saihakkō shite hoshii n da kedo...
want reissued   (explan.-is) but
"Uhh ... I lost my passport, and I'd like to get it reissued ..." (PL2)

- *funshitsu suru* is a rather formal word for "lose." A more colloquial word is *nakusu*.

Lesson 22 • The Wide World of *Desu*

One of the first things students of Japanese learn is that *desu* means "am/is/are," as in *Kore wa MANGAJIN desu*, "This is MANGAJIN." In relatively quick order they learn that *desu* can follow adjectives as well, as in *MANGAJIN wa omoshiroi desu*, "MANGAJIN is fun/interesting." Then somewhere along the line they might learn that, in the right context, they can also say *Watashi wa MANGAJIN desu*, which looks very much like "I am MANGAJIN," without eliciting snickers.

The use of *desu* in Japanese is quite a bit broader than (or at least it spreads across very different territory from) the use of the verb "to be" in English, and that is what makes it possible for a person to say *Watashi wa MANGAJIN desu*, for example, in a situation where he is being asked to make a choice. Depending on exactly what kind of choice is being made, the situation changes the meaning of the sentence to "I select/I vote for/I want/I will buy MANGAJIN" (nothing subliminal here).

In such cases the meaning is usually clear from the context, and most students have little difficulty comprehending, but it's a little more difficult to know when you can, or even should, use *desu* instead of a more active verb to make your Japanese sound natural. For that reason, in this lesson we focus on situations where English speakers might not think of using *desu*. We need to caution that it's not something that works by formula, so you will need to keep your ear tuned to what native speakers are saying. Hopefully the examples we present will help you get your ear tuned in the right direction.

All of the examples we've chosen have some kind of a noun followed by *desu* — or *da*, its PL2 equivalent — and in each case *desu* means more than just "am/is/are." Stretching for a single principle that pulls them all together, we could say that the noun in each case describes a situation or condition that applies to the speaker or to the person being spoken of. Even though many of the examples use the PL2 *da*, don't forget that in most cases the PL3 *desu* is the safer choice unless you're really sure it's a situation where you can be informal.

We begin with three examples in which an American speaker is likely to say "have."

Describing a person's condition or situation

The man was having trouble finding the right words, and the woman started to get her hopes up. But instead of confessing his love or proposing, he tells her he has AIDS — using *desu*. It's a situation where an English speaker would expect to use the verb "have," but to use *motte-iru* ("have/carry"), *aru* ("have/exists/there is"), or any of the many other equivalents an English-Japanese dictionary gives for "have" would sound odd in this case.

Man: ボク は エイズ です。
boku wa eizu desu.
I/me as-for AIDS am → have
"I have AIDS." (PL3)

"Sound" FX: ダッ
Da!
(effect of dashing away as fast as she can)

© Imazeki Shin / *O-jama Shimasu*, Take Shobō

136

With the explanatory *na no*

Explaining that he has a date tomorrow, Tanaka-kun is about to ask his friend a favor. The explanatory *no* becomes *na no* when it directly follows a noun like this.

© Tanaka Hiroshi / *Tanaka-kun*, Take Shobō

Tanaka-kun: 明日　デート　なん　だ　けど　さー
Ashita　dēto　na n　da　kedo　sā
Tomorrow　date　(explan.)　is　but/and　(emph.)
"I have a date tomorrow, and . . ." (PL2)

Friend: おっ!　カノジョ　できた　のか?
O!　Kanojo　dekita　no ka?
oh　girlfriend　was made　(explan.-?)
"Oh! Did you make/find a girlfriend?" (PL2)

- the conjunction *kedo* literally means "but," but when used at the end of a sentence this way (to set up background information and lead to the next part of the conversation), it functions like the English "and."
- *kanojo* is actually a pronoun for "she/her," but it is also used colloquially as a common noun meaning "girlfriend."

Making a choice

In a coffee shop the waiter comes to take their orders. There are of course other ways to place an order, but this *Edokko* ("child of Edo" → "native Tokyoite") uses one of the simplest ways to state his choice. Stating a personal choice or position can be thought of as a variation of describing one's own situation.

Waiter: ご注文　は?
Go-chūmon　wa?
(hon.)-order　as for
"Your order?" (PL3-4 implied)

Man: おいら　ブラジル　だ。
Oira　Burajiru　da.
I/me　Brazil　am/will be → will have
"I'll have Brazilian." (PL2)

- *oira* is a masculine slang word for "I/me," a somewhat softer variation of the rough *ore*.

© Tachibanaya Kikutarō / *Beranmei Tōchan*, Take Shobō

Telling someone where you are

A place name followed by *da/desu* is a common way of indicating where someone is — including where the speaker himself is when talking on the phone. In this example, the first *desu* is a standard "is/are," but the second one means "[you] are at/in . . ." Words like *ima* ("now"), *mada* ("now still"), and *mō* ("now already") are often included in such sentences. Here, Department Head Haruyama has inadvertently spoken with disrespect to the president of the company over the phone, and the shock of realizing his mistake has put him in a daze.

© Yamasaki & Kitami / *Tsuri-Baka Nisshi*, Shogakukan

Haruyama: 私　　は　　誰?　今、どこ?
Watashi wa dare? Ima, doko?
I/me　as-for who　now where
"Who am I? Where (am I) now?" (PL2)

Subordinates: 春山　　　　部長　　です。
Haruyama Buchō desu.
(name)　department head　are
"You are Department Head Haruyama." (PL3)

今　　会社　　　デース!!、
Ima kaisha de–su!!
now company/office/work are at
"Right now you are at the office." (PL2)

• *kaisha* is literally "company/firm" but is often used in situations where it is more natural to say "the office" or "work" in English.

Asking where someone is

You can ask someone's whereabouts by using the same pattern in a question. The gourmet seen here has just sampled a new dish developed by Mr. Sanjay and he wishes to know the whereabouts of the chef so that he can offer his compliments.

© Okazaki Jirō / *Afutā Zero*, Shogakukan

Gourmet: 素晴らしい　出来栄え　です　ね。
Subarashii dekibae desu ne.
wonderful　workmanship is/are (colloq.)
"Wonderfully executed." (PL3)

Gourmet: サンジェ氏　は　まだ　厨房　ですか?
Sanje-shi wa mada chūbō desu ka?
Sanjay Mr.　as-for still　kitchen　is
"Is Mr. Sanjay still in the kitchen?" (PL3)

• *dekibae* refers to how well something has been made: "workmanship/manner of execution."
• *chūbō* is a word for "kitchen" that has a certain archaic and/or aristocratic flavor. The more common word today is 台所 *daidokoro*, or even キッチン *kitchin*, from the English word.

Butler: 今、　お呼びします。
Ima, o-yobi shimasu.
now (hon.)-call/summon
"I will call him right away." (PL3-4)

• *o-yobi shimasu* is a polite/humble form of *yobu* ("call/summon").

Asking where someone is going

A place name followed by *da/desu* is also a way to say where a person is about to go instead of where he is at the moment. In this scene Kōsuke asks the student who lives in the apartment next door if he is going to school.

© Maekawa Tsukasa / *Dai-Tōkyō Binbō Seikatsu Manyuaru*, Kōdansha

Kōsuke: 学校　ですか?
Gakkō desu ka?
school　is it
"Off to school?" (PL3)

Student: ラグビー の　早慶戦　　見て、
Ragubii no Sōkei-sen mite,
rugby　of　Waseda-Keiō game　watch-and

そのあと コンパ なん です。
sono ato konpa na n desu.
afterward　party (explan.) is
"I'm going to watch the Waseda-Keiō rugby game, and afterwards there's a party." (PL3)

- *Sōkei* is made up of the first characters of 早稲田 Waseda and 慶応 Keiō, the two top private universities in Tokyo, and traditional sports rivals.
- drinking is usually the primary activity at a *konpa*. The generic word パーティー *pātii* is also used in Japanese.

For an action about to occur

When *desu* follows an action noun it can indicate that you are about to begin that action/ activity. Such sentences often start with an expression that implies impending action, such as *sā* ("well now"), *sassoku* ("immediately/right away"), *mō sugu* ("soon"), *ima kara* ("from now"), etc. These two innocent-looking characters are contemplating some mischief upon a *yakuza* ("gangster") they have been observing.

© Nakagawa Isami / *Kuma no Pūtarō*, Shogakukan

Nobuo: 真空 だ と どー かな?
Shinkū da to dō ka na?
vacuum is if how/what I wonder
"What would happen if (we put him in) a vacuum, I wonder?" (PL3)

Pūtarō: さっそく　実験 だ!
Sassoku jikken da!
right away experiment is
"Let's do an experiment right away!" (PL2)

As a kind of shorthand . . . for wearing something

***Da/desu* after almost any noun** can serve as a kind of shorthand to indicate an action associated with that object. From the few examples that we present here you can probably see that the possibilities of what *da/desu* can stand for are nearly unlimited. In this first case, *da* effectively means "wear."

© Nōjō / *Muryoku no Ō*, Shogakukan

Buchō: おはよ!!
Ohayo!!
"Mornin'!!"

Sound FX: ボン
Bon
Thump (effect of a solid slap on her back)

OL: 部長!!
Buchō!!
"Chief!!" (PL3)

- a *buchō* is a department head in a company.

Chief: 由紀ちゃん は いつも ブレザー だ ね。 暑くない かい?!
Yuki-chan wa itsumo burezā da ne. Atsukunai kai?
(name-dimin.) as-for always blazer is/are (colloq.) not hot (?)
"Yuki-chan, you always wear a blazer, don't you? Aren't you hot?" (PL2)

- *kai* is a masculine colloquial version of the question marker *ka*. It sounds less abrupt than *ka* in this kind of usage.

. . . for riding a bicycle

Kōsuke and Hiroko were at a bar, where just two drinks put Kōsuke to sleep. Now Hiroko is seeing him home. As they come out of the train station, Kōsuke remembers that he rode his bicycle.

© Maekawa Tsukasa / *Dai-Tōkyō Binbō Seikatsu Manyuaru*, Kōdansha

Kōsuke: あ。
A.
"Oh."

Kōsuke: 自転車 なん だ。
Jitensha na n da.
bicycle (explan.) is
"I rode my bike." (PL2)

Sound FX: ガチャ
Gacha
(clicking of the bicycle lock)

. . . for taking vacation

Sarari-kun rejoices on the day before his vacation starts, declaring himself synonymous with "summer vacation." What he means, of course, is that he will be on vacation starting the next day.

© Nishimura Sō / *Sarari-kun*

Sarari-kun:
明日　から　オレ　は　　　夏休み　だーッ。
Ashita　kara　ore　wa　natsu-yasumi　da—!
tomorrow from　I/me　as-for summer vaction　am
"From tomorrow I go on summer vacation."
(PL2)

Sarari-kun:　海　へ！　山　へ！
Umi　e!　Yama　e!
ocean to　mountain to
"To the beach! To the mountains!"

. . . for saying "goodbye"

This one is a little different from our other "shorthand" examples, but it still fits that description. In Lesson 11 we introduced *O-saki ni shitsurei shimasu* (literally, "I will do the rudeness of leaving first/before you") as the appropriate way to say "good-bye" when leaving the office before your co-workers. One of several ways to shorten that "goodbye" is the way this OL does when her boss tells her he has to stay to finish up a little more work.

© Wakabayashi Kenji / *Heisei Arashiyama Ikka*, Shogakukan

OL:　そいじゃ　お先　　です。
Soi ja　o-saki　desu.
in that case (hon.)-first/before am/is
"Well, then, goodbye." (PL3 informal)

- *soi ja* is a contraction of *sore de wa,* "in that case/well then."

Lesson 23 • *Hai* (Part I)

As a rule, a word in one language rarely has a truly exact equivalent in another language; there are always differences, though often very subtle ones, in nuance and usage. Still, with words as simple and basic as *hai* and "yes," one might expect to find exceptions to the rule.

No such luck. *Hai* and "yes" do indeed cover a lot of the same territory, but *hai* in Japanese is also used in some situations where an English speaker would rarely or never say "yes." In fact the uses of *hai* are sufficiently varied, and sufficiently different from the usage of "yes" in English, that we have decided to devote two lessons to them.

For this first lesson we have chosen examples in which *hai* means "yes" in the sense of affirmation: answering a yes-or-no question, confirming the truth/correctness of something, or assenting/agreeing to do what another person has asked. For the most part, these represent situations where the correspondence between *hai* and "yes" is quite close: either "Yes" by itself is a fully adequate translation, or it can be worked into a phrase like "Yes, that is correct," or "Yes, I will do as you wish." But in some of the examples it seems less strained simply to consider *hai* as equivalent to "okay/all right/certainly." And then there are the cases where *hai* in response to negative questions seems to mean "no" instead of "yes."

In the next lesson we will feature examples in which *hai* means "yes" in the sense of "I hear you" (with various additional implications depending on the circumstance), and some other miscellaneous uses.

In business negotiations, there have been cases in which Americans accused the Japanese of backing out on what the Americans thought was a done deal, and even when matters don't reach that point, Americans often express their exasperation at not being able to tell when "yes" means "yes" to the Japanese. In some cases the problem is no doubt with American misunderstanding of *hai*, while in others it is with Japanese misuse of "yes" as if it were an exact equivalent of *hai*. We hope this two-part lesson will give our readers a better grasp of the important differences between *hai* and "yes."

A plain "Yes" or "No" question

In this scene from *Sasayama-san,* the *buchō* ("division head") has just finished apologizing for abruptly canceling what was to be Sasayama's first-ever golfing experience the day before. Now he wants to know if Sasayama would be free to join him in entertaining a client tonight.

©Yamasaki and Kitami / *Sasayama san,* Shogakukan

Buchō: ところで
Tokoro-de
by the way

今夜　は　　あいてる　か　ね?
kon'ya wa　　aite-ru　ka　ne?
tonight as-for　open　　?　(colloq.)
"By the way, are you free tonight?"
(PL2)

Sasayama: はい。
Hai.
"Yes." (PL3)

• *aite-(i)ru* ("be open/free") is from *aku* ("[something] opens/becomes free").

142

A negative question

Negative questions are sometimes tricky because the logic is different from that in English. The general rule to remember is that answering *Hai* essentially means "Yes, that negative statement is correct." As this example shows, *Hai* would actually correspond to an English "No" in such cases.

In this scene Shōsuke has been waiting to hear from another section chief, Kozuka, in the same food products division of Itsui Bussan, a huge trading company. Because of the intense rivalry between these sections, it turns out that Kozuka has "stolen" customers from Shōsuke's section.

© Hijiri Hideo / *Naze ka Shōsuke*, Shogakukan

<u>Takayama:</u> 3日　も　たつ　のに、
Mikka　mo　tatsu　no ni,
three days　all of　pass　even though

小塚課長　　から 何も 言ってきてないの!?
Kozuka-kachō kara　nani mo itte kite-nai no!?
(name-title)　　from　　haven't said a thing
"It's been three whole days, and Mr. Kozuka hasn't gotten back to you at all?" (PL2)

<u>Shōsuke:</u> ハイッ。
Hai!
"Yes (that is correct)" → **"No, he hasn't."** (PL3)

- *mo* after *mikka* ("three days") indicates that, in this case, three days is a long time.

<u>Shōsuke:</u> しかし、小塚課長　　は　　一昨日　　　から 北海道　へ　出張　　です し、
Shikashi, Kozuka-kachō wa　ototoi　　kara Hokkaidō e　shutchō　desu shi . . .
however, (name-title)　as-for day before yesterday from Hokkaidō to business trip is　and
"But, Mr. Kozuka has been on a business trip to Hokkaido since the day before yesterday, and . . ." (PL2)

- the kanji 一昨日 can be read *ototoi* (conversational), or *issakujitsu* (formal).
- Shōsuke, the eternal optimist, is trying to rationalize the fact that he has not heard back from Kozuka-kachō about some prospective customers he has found for a new product. Takayama, on the other hand, suspects that Kozuka-kachō's silence is a bad sign.

An ordinary request

The president of a moving company is asking the clerk to show him some order slips. The question here uses an ordinary, positive verb form, and the *Hai* response is straightforward, just like a "Yes" in English.

© Hosano Fujihiko / *Gallery Fake*, Shogakukan

President: ちょっと 受注票 を 見せてくれる か？
Chotto juchū-hyō o misete kureru ka?
a little order slips (obj.) show me ?
"Would you let me see those order slips a minute?" (PL2)

Clerk: はい。
Hai.
"Yes, sir." (PL3)

A request with a negative wording

The general rule regarding negative questions and *hai* does not hold when the negative question is an invitation or request. Invitations are normally made in a negative form (*-nai ka/-masen ka* = "won't you . . ."), while making a request with *-te kurenai ka* ("won't you [please] . . . for me?"), like the teacher in this example, is really just a way of making the request sound "gentler"/more polite, rather than being a true negative statement. In either case, answering *hai* expresses acceptance/assent: "certainly/all right."

© Akiyama Jyōji / *Haguregumo*, Shogakukan

Teacher: 新之助。
Shinnosuke.
(name)

今度 お父上 に あわせてくれないか。
Kondo o-chichiue ni awasete kurenai ka?
this time (hon.)-father with won't you let me meet (please)?
"Shinnosuke. Won't you let me meet your father sometime?" (PL2)

Shinnosuke: は, はい。
Ha, hai.
okay/sure
"O- okay." (PL3)

- *chichiue* is a word for "father" that has an archaic/aristocratic feeling — appropriate for the setting of this story.
- *awasete* is from *awaseru*, the causative "make/let –" form of *au* ("meet").

Asking permission

At a *ryōtei* (a high class restaurant) this Chairman of the Board wants to show his subordinate how intimate/familiar he is with the proprietress, and asks if he can lay his head on her lap. She grants him permission by responding with *Hai hai*.

© Nitta Tatsuo / *Torishimariyaku Hira Namijiro,* Shogakukan

Chairman: 久し振りに　　　　　深酒　して、
Hisashiburi ni   fukazake shite
for first time in long time heavy drinking did-and
眠く　なってきた　わい。
nemuku natte kita   wai.
sleepy   am becoming (masc. colloq.)
"I've drunk more than I have in a long time, and I'm getting sleepy." (PL2)

いいかな，女将?
Ii ka na, Okami?
fine/okay is it
"May I, Madam?" (PL2)

Proprietress: はいはい。
Hai hai.
"Yes, yes (go ahead)."

Clarifying a response

From *Oishinbo:* the impetuous reporter, Yamaoka, invites his female co-worker, Kurita, to a restaurant. Although there is undeniably an attraction between these two, Yamaoka's pride will not allow him to show any sign of affection. This is how he reacts after Kurita mentions another man she has been seeing.

© Kariya Tetsu and Hanasaki Akira / *Oishinbo,* Shogakukan

Yamaoka: 来る　の？　来ない　の？
Kuru no? Konai   no?
come (ques.) not come (ques.)
"Are you coming or not?" (PL2)

Kurita: はい　はい。
Hai   hai.
yes   yes
行きます、行きます。
Ikimasu,   ikimasu.
(I will) go   (I will) go
"Okay okay. I'm coming, I'm coming." (PL3)

- you could say that her *"Hai"* was a response to the positive part of his question; or, you could say that the *"Hai"* was more an acknowledgment of the question, with *"Ikimasu"* being the actual response. In either case, clarifying the response with a statement of what you intend to do is a good idea in this case, since it could be confusing even to native speakers.
- note the use of the verb *iku* ("go") in a situation where an English speaker would say "come."

An exception?

In this scene, from *Sanchōme no Yūhi*, the boy recognizes his old childhood sweetheart on the university campus where they are both students. They were separated during elementary school when his father was transferred to another town.

In the second frame, his question appears to be a negative one, but the actual thought process here could be called positive — he thinks that it probably <u>is</u> his old sweetheart, and he wants to verify that. Contrast this with the negative question in our second example in which Takayama thinks that Kozuka probably has <u>not</u> gotten back to Shōsuke.

Since the response to this kind of question can be confusing even to native speakers, she clarifies her response by stating her name.

Fumio: あのう...もしもし。
Anō...   Moshi moshi.
Uhh...   Hello
"Uhh . . . Excuse me."

Miko: は、はい...?
Ha, hai?
"Ye- yes?"

- *moshi moshi* is best known to students of Japanese as a way of answering the telephone. The usage shown here, as a way of hailing or attracting another person's attention, might seem a little old-fashioned, but is not unusual.
- her response of *Hai* here is more along the lines of the examples we will present in the next lesson — acknowledging that you hear the other person.

© Saigan Ryōhei / *Sanchōme no Yūhi*, Shogakukan

Fumio: 失礼   です けど、
Shitsurei desu kedo,
impolite   is   but

日辺美子さん   じゃないですか?
Nippen Miko-san   ja nai desuka?
(name-hon.)   aren't you
"I beg your pardon, but aren't you Nippen Miko?" (PL3)

Miko: は、はい。日辺 ですけど、あなたは?
Ha, hai. Nippen desu kedo, anata wa?
ye, yes   (name) am   but   you as-for
"Ye- yes, my name is Nippen, but who are you?" (PL3)

- a more conventional reading for her name would be Hinabe Yoshiko. This story is about her problems with writing, however, so the name Nip<u>pen</u> is a pun of sorts.

(continued from p. 41)
skewer of vegetables, so he said *Yao kudasai* (八百下さい). Of course, he should have said *Yasai kudasai* （野菜下さい）, but he had learned the connection between the ending -*ya* and shops selling various items. For example, he knew that a *sakana-ya* (魚屋) sold fish (*sakana*), and a *kutsu-ya* (靴屋) sold shoes (*kutsu*), so he thought that since a *yaoya* (八百屋) sold vegetables, *yao* must be the word for vegetables."

• From a source wishing to remain anonymous: "A Japanese friend and I were waiting for a bus which was long overdue. I knew that the English word 'bus' was used in Japanese but I went by the English spelling and said *Busu ga konai ne* (ブスが来ないね, 'The *busu* doesn't come, does it'). After my friend stopped laughing, she explained that *busu* is a slang word for an unattractive female. The word 'bus' is rendered as バス (*basu*) in Japanese, closer to the English pronunciation than the English spelling."

• A reader in Nagoya recalls: "Despite having lived in Japan for two years, I have never acquired a taste for that ubiquitous drink known as お茶 (*o-cha*, "Japanese tea"), though I do like certain other forms of tea that are available in Japan. Once I was explaining this to a Japanese friend and told her that I liked oolong-*cha*, mugi-*cha*, and *shitagi-cha*. At this she raised a quizzical eyebrow and asked what *shitagi-cha* was. I explained that it was a tea made from mushrooms, which I had enjoyed once in Nagano Prefecture. My friend let out a great howl of laughter and informed me that the word was *shiitake* (椎茸). *Shitagi* (下着) is "underwear.""

• Anonymous: "We were having dinner in a restaurant in Japan and the chef came out to see how we liked the food. He asked *Ikaga desu ka* (いかがですか), meaning 'How is it (the food),' but I had learned *Ikaga desu ka* as a way of asking 'How are you?' Looking back, I recall that he did smile when I replied *Genki desu* (元気です, 'I'm fine'), but it was only later that I was let in on the joke."

• The setting was a speech in front of a PTA group. The foreign speaker wanted to say that the grass at home was a different color from the grass of Japan. Instead of 草 (*kusa*, "grass"), the word that came out was くそ (*kuso*), or, politely put, "excrement." The most amusing part was that the mothers only nodded their heads and muttered *Ah, sō desu ka?* (ああそうですか, "Is that so?").

• An American reader in Japan listened to his radio from time to time for language practice. One morning, he heard his first Japanese weather report: *Ichiji ame ga furu desho.* Meeting with a friend around noon, he remarked, "The weather forecasting system here is certainly advanced. They are predicting rain at one o'clock." His friend laughed and informed him that *ichiji,* which does mean "one o'clock," has a meaning of "occasionally" in this context.

• "After lunch, I always go to my university's co-op store (生協, *seikyō*)," relates a student in Fukuoka. "I thought the cashier in the store was really nice and polite because she always asked me *Genki desu ka?* (元気ですか, 'Are you well/How are you doing?') when I stopped to pay. I always answered, *Genki desu, arigatō gozaimasu* (元気です、ありがとうございます, 'Fine, thank you.') I finally realized that she was actually asking '*Genkin desu ka*,' (現金ですか, 'Will it be cash?'). Now I know why she was always smiling at me!"

Lesson 24 • *Hai* (Part 2)

In Lesson 23, we looked at examples in which *hai* meant "yes" in an affirmative sense: answering a yes-or-no question (*hai* = a straightforward "yes"), confirming the truth/correctness of something (*hai* = "yes, that is correct," including the confusing case in which *hai* seems to mean "no"), or assenting/agreeing to do what another person had asked (*hai* = "yes, I will do as you ask"). In several cases, especially in the last group, the use of *hai* generally corresponded more closely with words like "okay/all right/sure/certainly" than with the way we use "yes" in English.

In this lesson we begin with a number of examples showing *hai* used to mean "I hear/heard you." Since the English "yes" (or "yeah/uh-huh") is used in the same way to some extent, this use of *hai* can also be translated as "yes" — sometimes.

Since *hai* essentially belongs to PL3, it is the "safe" word for "yes/okay/sure," which can be used without fear of offending anyone. When you are in situations where you know it's okay to be less formal, you can replace *hai* with *ee* ("yes") or *un* ("yeah/uh-huh") in cases like the first five examples (though it would not be appropriate when answering the phone). In the other cases this substitution is not possible.

As usual, we can't claim to have illustrated all of the uses of *hai*, even in a two-part lesson, but we hope you find this extended treatment helpful in understanding how to use *hai* more effectively and naturally.

"I hear you and I understand"

Having heard his boss tell the secretary that he will be out until about 3:00, Tanaka-kun decides he will go out until about 2:30. When he informs the secretary of his plans, she acknowledges his statement with a *Hai* — just as she did the boss's — essentially meaning "I hear you and I understand/I get the message."

© Tanaka Hiroshi / *Tanaka-kun*, Take Shobō

Tanaka-kun: 島田さん、　　ちょっと　　外出　　　して　　　くる　から。
Shimada-san,　chotto　gaishutsu　shite　kuru　kara.
(name)　　a little while　outing　will do/go on-and　come　so
"Miss Shimada, I'll be going out for awhile." (PL2)

Miss Shimada: はい。
Hai.
"Okay." (PL3)

- *gaishutsu* = "an outing" and *gaishutsu suru* = "go out"; the word implies a return, but adding *kuru* ("come") makes the return explicit.

"I hear you and I'm listening"

These women have already been talking for a while, but now the woman in the first frame wants to broach a new point. As she begins, she pauses with a *ne* after *watashi* to make sure that Sakurako will pay particular attention to what she is about to say next. Sakurako confirms she is listening by saying *Hai*. Seeking and giving feedback like this is a standard part of truly natural Japanese speech.

© Takeda & Takai / *Pro Golfer Oribe Kinjiroh*, Shogakukan

Sakurako: はい。
Hai.
"Yes?" (PL3)

- although an English "Yes?" would probably have a rising intonation, Sakurako's *hai* would be spoken with essentially flat intonation.

Woman: 桜子さん . . .   私 ね . . .
Sakurako-san . . . Watashi ne . . .
(name-hon.)   I/me   (colloq.)
"Sakurako . . . I . . ." (PL3)

- the suffix *-san* added to people's names is used with first (given) names quite a bit more than English "Miss/Ms./Mr."

"Hello (I'm listening)"

Answering the phone with a *Hai* can be considered a special case of the "I hear you and I'm listening" category. It may be stretching things a bit to say that *Hai* actually means "Hello" in such cases, since English speakers also sometimes answer the phone with "Yes?" But we can probably say that Japanese speakers use *Hai* as a "Hello" more often than English speakers use "Yes?" for that purpose. The second and third *Hai*s in this example are simply an indication to the other party that he is (attentively) listening. This practice of providing verbal confirmation that communication is going smoothly is called *aizuchi*.

© Yamamoto Terry / *Bow-wow*, Shogakukan

Kuramoto: ハイ 倉本 です。
Hai Kuramoto desu.
"Hello. Kuramoto here." (PL3)

ハイ . . . ハイ!?
Hai . . . Hai
"Yes . . . Yes!?"

- *ee* or *un* cannot normally be used instead of *hai* when answering the phone. They can be used just like *hai* for *aizuchi*, to continually signal "I'm still listening." Kuramoto is an aspiring manga artist, and this is a call from a publisher, so he uses the more formal *Hai*.
- the last *hai* could be translated as, "Huh?" — his response to a demanding deadline.
- in case you are wondering why he is wiping his cheek, his dog was licking his face just before the phone rang.

"I heard you and I will respond."

In these two examples, *hai* is not the actual response, it's just an indication that the question was understood and that a response is forthcoming. In some cases it serves as a kind of hesitation word, giving a few moments to decide how to answer.

In this first scene, Miss Sonoda wants to be admitted to college through the usual exams rather than on the strength of her performance as a track athlete. She went to a cram school for a mock exam to evaluate her chances, but the results were not encouraging.

© Saimon Fumi / *Asunaro Hakusho*, Shogakukan

Coach: で　園田、
De　Sonoda,
and so　(name)

予備校　　行ってみて　　どう　だった?
yobikō　　itte mite　　dō　datta?
cram school　go/went to see-and　how　was it
"So Sonoda, how did things go at the cram school?" (PL2)

Sonoda: はい。
Hai.
"Well . . ." (PL3)

• the particle *e*, to indicate destination, has been omitted after *yobikō* ("cram school").

In a large trading company, one section (headed by Kozuka) has developed a "boil in bag" pack of rice. In this scene, Ōhara, from another section, is trying to get some of the product for his customers. Because of inter-section rivalry, Kozuka charges Ōhara a much higher price and winds up trying to steal his customers.

© Hijiri Hideo / *Naze ka Shōsuke*, Shogakukan

Kozuka: どれ　くらいの　　量　　が　ほしいの　か　ね、　大原クン。
Dore　kurai no　ryō　ga　hoshii no　ka　ne,　Ōhara-kun.
about　how much　quantity　(subj.)　is wanted　(?)　(colloq.)　(name-hon.)
"What kind of quantity do you want, Ōhara?" (PL2)

Ohara: ハイッ。
Hai!
"Well, (sir)." (PL3)

• in the next panel Ōhara actually states the quantity he needs.

"I hear the bell and I'm coming"

It's customary to call out an elongated *ha–i,* in a raised voice, as one hurries to answer the door-bell. In fact, the raised voice and elongated vowel seem to be fairly standard in any situation where one is being called to the phone, to the front door, to another room, etc. — oftentimes even when the distance is close enough that a raised voice is not strictly necessary.

© Hoshizato Mochiru / *Ribingu Gēmu,* Shogakukan

Sound FX: ふーっ ふーっ
Fū! Fū!
(effect of blowing on her skinned knee, to which she has just applied an antiseptic)

Sound FX: ピンポーン
Pin pōn
Ding do-n-ng (sound of door chimes)

Izumi: はーい。
Ha—i.
"Com-i-ing." (PL2)

"I heard you and I don't want to hear any more."

Granny isn't happy about the way her grandson is going about getting married, and insists that he must at least formally register the marriage on a day designated as *taian* (大安, an "auspicious day" according to ancient Chinese divination practices). She has obviously given her grandson an earful even before this outburst, and this time he cuts her off.

© Rokuda Noboru / *Efu,* Shogakukan

Granny:
当たり前 じゃ!
Atarimae ja!
of course is
"Of course (I want you to do it on an auspicious day)!" (PL2)

式 も あげん、 新婚旅行 に も いかん、
Shiki mo agen, shinkon ryokō ni mo ikan,
ceremony even not hold honeymoon on also not go
"You don't hold a ceremony, you don't take a honeymoon, . . ."

せめて 婚姻届 ぐらい 大安の日に 出さんと . . .
semete kon'in todoke gurai taian no hi ni dasan to . . .
at least marriage registration at least on auspicous day if don't submit
"(so) if you don't at least submit your marriage registration on an auspicious day . . ."

この 一生 に 一度 の 特別な—
kono isshō ni ichido no tokubetsu-na
this one life in one time 's special
"then this once-in-a-lifetime special . . ." (PL2)

• *agen = agenai,* negative of *ageru* ("hold [a wedding]"); *ikan = ikanai,* negative of *iku* ("go"); and *dasan = dasanai,* negative of *dasu* ("put out/submit").

Grandson: はい はい はい はい。
Hai, hai, hai, hai.
"Yeah, yeah, yeah, yeah." (PL1)

"Here" when handing something over

In this large automotive company, people go to *sōmu* (総務, "general affairs") to get office supplies. In this kind of situation, *hai* corresponds to "Here (you are)" in English.

© Hayashi & Takai / *Yamaguchi Roppeita*, Shogakukan

Clerk: はい、　マジック　に　ボールペン。
Hai,　majikku　ni　bōrupen.
okay/here magic marker(s) and ballpoint pen(s)
"Here you are, magic markers and ballpoint pens." (PL2)

Worker: どうも。
Dōmo.
indeed/very much
"Thanks." (PL2)

- *dōmo*, meaning "indeed/really/quite," is added to a number of expressions to make them more emphatic, but it's also used as a shortened form of those expressions. In this case, it's short for *Dōmo arigatō (gozaimasu)*, "Thank you very much."

To direct someone's attention

This person standing outside the club/cabaret is called a *kyaku-hiki* (客引き, literally "customer-puller"). Customers are typically addressed as *Okyaku-san* ("[hon.]-Mr./Ms. Customer"), so using this term for someone just walking down the street is a kind of "positive thinking" by the *kyaku-hiki*.

© Takeda & Takai / *Pro Golfer Oribe Kinjiroh*, Shogakukan

Kyaku-hiki: はい、　お客さん、　いらっしゃい。
Hai,　okyaku-san,　irasshai.
okay/yes (hon.)-customer step in/welcome
"Yes sir, right this way." (PL2)

Sign: ショークラブ　あすか
Shō Kurabu　Asuka
Show Club Asuka

A signal to begin

Hai can be used like "Okay, go/start" to signal when an action should begin. Often, the action to be done is indicated in a command form right after *hai*, as in this scene where a singer has come to be examined by an ear, nose, and throat specialist.

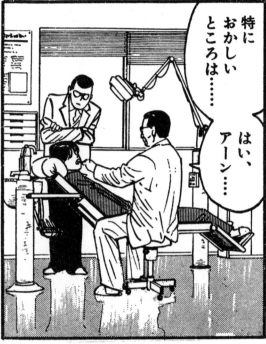

© Tsuchida Seiki / *Orebushi,* Shogakukan

Doctor: 特に　　　　　　　　おかしい　　ところ　　は？
Toku ni　　　　okashii　　tokoro　　wa?
especially/particularly strange/abnormal place/point as-for
"Any particular problems?" (PL2)

はい、アーン。
Hai,　　ān.
okay　(effect of wide open mouth)
"Okay, open wide please." (PL2)

- *okashii* means "strange/unusual/abnormal," and *tokoro* (literally "place") is often used to mean "matter/point of concern." When speaking of health, *okashii tokoro* means "health problem/complaint."
- in this case the topic particle *wa* is all that's needed to imply the question, "Do you have . . . ?"
- the FX word *ān*, representing a wide open mouth, is commonly used as a command by dentists, mothers feeding babies, and others who want you to open your mouth for some reason.

A signal to end

Hai can also signal the end of an action. A tailor has been taking a customer's measurements for a suit. Here he uses *hai* to let the customer know that he is finished.

© Oikawa Kōji / *Kachō ni Kampai,* Jitsugyō no Nihonsha

Tailor: はい、いい　　でしょ。
Hai,　ii　　　desho.
okay good/enough probably/should be
"Okay, that should do it." (PL3)

A

間	*aida*	interval, p. 29
相手	*aite*	other party/opponent, p. 87
あん	*an*	bean jam, p. 38
暗証番号	*anshō bangō*	secret code number, p. 65
洗う	*arau*	wash (*v.*), p. 72
あした	*ashita*	tomorrow, p. 27, 92, 137, 141
会う	*au*	meet, p. 92, 132, 104, 144

B

黴菌	*baikin*	germ/bacteria, p. 38
馬鹿	*baka*	fool/foolishness, p. 66-71, 98
馬鹿な	*baka-na*	crazy/foolish/stupid, p. 67
バカにする	*baka ni suru*	make fun of, p. 70
罰金	*bakkin*	fine/penalty, p. 20
バス	*basu*	bus, p. 147
ベンピ	*benpi*	constipation, p. 47
ビデオ	*bideo*	video, p. 52, 104
ビーフ味	*biifu-aji*	beef-flavored, p. 85
美人	*bijin*	beautiful woman, p. 58
貧乏	*binbō*	poverty, p. 40
坊	*bō*	(Buddhist) priest, p. 48
僕	*boku*	I/me (*masc.*), p. 61, 80, 136
ボーナス	*bōnasu*	bonus, p. 99
ボールペン	*bōrupen*	ballpoint pen(s), p. 152
ブラジル	*Burajiru*	Brazil, p. 137
無沙汰する	*busata suru*	neglect to call/write/visit, p. 56

C

お茶	*o-cha*	(green) tea, p. 61, 62, 79, 133, 147
地球	*chikyū*	Earth, p. 107
ちょっと	*chotto*	a little/slightly, p. 64, 73, 76, 81, 92, 100, 131, 148
厨房	*chūbō*	kitchen (formal), p. 138
ご注文	*go-chūmon*	(an) order/request, p. 137

D

台所	*daidokoro*	kitchen, p. 138
暖房器	*danbōki*	heater, p. 64
誰	*dare*	who (informal), p. 50, 138
出来栄え	*dekibae*	workmanship/result, p. 138
電話	*denwa*	telephone, p. 14, 104
電話番号	*denwa bangō*	telephone number, p. 117
どこ	*doko*	where, p. 138
どこか	*doko ka*	somewhere, p. 87
どく	*doku*	get out of the way/make room for, p. 20
どなた	*donata*	who (polite), p. 77

E

エイズ	*eizu*	AIDS, p. 136

F

深酒	*fukazake*	heavy drinking, p. 145
福	*fuku*	(good) luck/fortune, p. 89
不滅の	*fumetsu no*	unbeatable/immortal, p. 105
紛失する	*funshitsu suru*	lose/misplace, p. 135
風鈴	*fūrin*	wind-chime, p. 30
古くさい	*furukusai*	old-fashioned, p. 30
フタ	*futa*	lid/cover/cap, p. 45
太る	*futoru*	become fat, p. 96

G

外出する	*gaishutsu suru*	go out, p. 148
学校	*gakkō*	school, p. 139
ガム	*gamu*	chewing gum, p. 85
合宿	*gasshuku*	retreat/training session, p. 104
月末	*getsumatsu*	end of the month, p. 27
午後	*gogo*	afternoon, p. 94
牛乳	*gyūnyū*	milk, p. 23

H

蝿	*hae*	fly/flies (*n.*), p. 81
ハエジゴク	*hae-jigoku*	Venus' flytrap, p. 81
母	*haha*	(my) mother, p. 22
初める	*hajimeru*	begin/start, p. 55, 118
計る	*hakaru*	measure (*v.*), p. 125
花婿	*hanamuko*	bridegroom, p. 45
犯罪	*hanzai*	crime/offense, p. 70
葉っぱ	*happa*	leaf/leaves, p. 102
晴れ	*hare*	clear (weather), p. 70
早い	*hayai*	early/quick/rapid, p. 14, 42, 43
ヒゲ	*hige*	whisker(s), p. 103
ひく	*hiku*	catch (a cold), p. 71
人質	*hitojichi*	hostage/prisoner, p. 52
ヒツジ	*hitsuji*	sheep, p. 106
ホームラン	*hōmuran*	(a) home run, p. 89, 105
保証人	*hoshōnin*	guarantor, p. 99

I

一番安い	*ichiban yasui*	cheapest, p. 23
いちご	*ichigo*	strawberry, p. 110
いなか者	*inakamono*	bumpkin/rustic/hick, p. 22
印鑑	*inkan*	seal/stamp, p. 124
一本足	*ippon-ashi*	one-legged, p. 105
いろ	*iro*	color(s), p. 35
いろいろ	*iro-iro*	various, p. 24
一生に一度	*isshō ni ichido*	once in a lifetime, p. 151
いつも	*itsumo*	always, p. 140
一等国	*ittō-koku*	world power/1st class country, p. 85
いよいよ	*iyo-iyo*	at last/finally, p. 113

J

じゃま	*jama*	nuisance/bother, p. 14, 57
地獄	*jigoku*	hell, p. 81
実験	*jikken*	experiment (*n.*), p. 139
自転車	*jitensha*	bicycle, p. 85, 111, 140
じつ	*jitsu*	reality, p. 29
受注票	*juchū-hyō*	order slips, p. 144
順番	*junban*	order/turn/sequence, p. 24

K

帰る	*kaeru*	return (home), p. 28, 80, 91, 94, 111

The Vocabulary Summary is taken from material appearing in this book. It's not always possible to give the complete range of meanings for a word in this limited space, so our "definitions" are based on the usage of the word in a particular example.

かえって	*kaette*	to the contrary, p. 30
会社	*kaisha*	company/office/work, p. 138
会社の経費	*kaisha no keihi*	company expense, p. 87
開始	*kaishi*	beginning/start, p. 49
かける	*kakeru*	call (on the phone), p. 77
構え	*kamae*	stance/posture, p. 105
神	*kami*	god(s), p. 89
お金	*o-kane*	money, p. 27
考える	*kangaeru*	think about/consider, p. 65
感じ	*kanji*	feeling/effect/impression, p. 116
韓国	*Kankoku*	Korea, p. 18
カノジョ	*kanojo*	girlfriend/she, p. 137
可能性	*kanōsei*	possibility/potential, p. 100
感心する	*kanshin suru*	be impressed, p. 88
顔	*kao*	face (*n.*), p. 106
彼氏	*kareshi*	boyfriend, p. 55, 123
菓子	*kashi*	candy/confection, p. 23
貸す	*kasu*	lend, p. 79
方	*kata*	person (hon.), p. 77
仇	*kataki*	revenge, p. 53
かわいい	*kawaii*	cute, p. 31
風邪	*kaze*	(a) cold, p. 71, 114
刑事	*keiji*	(police) detective, p. 52
結婚式	*kekkon-shiki*	wedding ceremony, p. 27
結婚する	*kekkon suru*	marry, p. 16
煙	*kemuri*	smoke (*n.*), p. 71
血圧	*ketsuatsu*	blood pressure, p. 125, 128
きれいな	*kirei-na*	pretty/neat/clean, p. 35, 50
気色悪い	*kishoku warui*	disgusting, p. 81
コーチ	*kōchi*	coach, p. 50
こちら	*kochira*	this way/direction, p. 17, 18, 23, 62, 66, 118, 120–122
交換	*kōkan*	exchange/trade (*n.*), p. 103
心地よい	*kokochi yoi*	comfortable/pleasant, p. 115
国際	*kokusai*	international, p. 91
今度	*kondo*	this time/soon, p. 16
婚姻届	*kon'in todoke*	marriage registration, p. 151
今夜	*kon'ya*	tonight, p. 142
交渉する	*kōshō suru*	negotiate, p. 87
こそ	*koso*	indeed/all the more, p. 17, 14, 82
こと	*koto*	thing/situation/arrangement, p. 47, 65, 69, 88, 100, 101
今年	*kotoshi*	this year, p. 17, 71
こわい	*kowai*	scary, p. 51
お小遣い	*o-kozukai*	spending money/allowance, p. 97
車	*kuruma*	car, p. 55, 79
靴屋	*kutsu-ya*	shoe store, p. 147
今日	*kyō*	today, p. 82, 94, 121

M

毎月	*maitsuki*	every month, p. 19
マジック	*majikku*	magic marker(s), p. 152
まったく	*mattaku*	completely/utterly/truly, p. 21
めでたい	*medetai*	joyous/auspicious, p. 42, 45
見本	*mihon*	example, p. 7
(お)見送り	*(o-)miokuri*	send-off, p. 51
認める	*mitomeru*	recognize/acknowledge, p. 87

| 見つける | *mitsukeru* | find, p. 45, 86 |
| 燃える | *moeru* | burn (*v.*), p. 51 |

N

流す	*nagasu*	wash away/scrub, p. 25
(お)名前	*(o-)namae*	name (*n.*), p. 132
なんだかんだ	*nanda-kanda*	this-and-that, p. 27
何か	*nani ka*	something, p. 81
なる	*naru*	become, p. 16, 27, 29, 101, 112
夏	*natsu*	summer, p. 29
夏休み	*natsu-yasumi*	summer vacation, p. 141
猫	*neko*	cat, p. 31, 69, 103
眠くなる	*nemuku naru*	become sleepy, p. 145
人間	*ningen*	human being, p. 69
日誌	*nisshi*	diary, p. 67
飲む	*nomu*	drink (*v.*), p. 60, 62, 79
ぬる	*nuru*	paint (*v.*), p. 35

O

踊る	*odoru*	dance (*v.*), p. 29
大げさな	*ōgesa-na*	exaggerated/inflated, p. 47
おかしい	*okashii*	strange/abnormal, p. 153
怒る	*okoru*	become angry, p. 81, 101
送ります	*okurimasu*	send, p. 15
奥さん	*okusan*	(someone else's) wife, p. 40
おもしろい	*omoshiroi*	interesting/amusing, p. 81
思う	*omou*	think, p. 18
おりる	*oriru*	get/come down, p. 21
幼なじみ	*osana-najimi*	childhood friend, p. 123
遅い	*osoi*	late/slow, p. 72, 111
一昨日	*ototoi*	day before yesterday, p. 143
終わる	*owaru*	finish/be over, p. 28

R

ラグビー	*ragubii*	rugby, p. 139
ライバル	*raibaru*	rival, p. 95
ラッキー	*rakkii*	lucky, p. 86
お礼	*o-rei*	fee/reward, p. 125
ロビー	*robii*	(hotel) lobby, p. 51
量	*ryō*	quantity, p. 150
良好な	*ryōkō-na*	good/favorable, p. 64
領収書	*ryōshūsho*	receipt, p. 65

S

再発行する	*saihakkō suru*	reissue, p. 135
魚	*sakana*	fish, p. 147
先に	*saki ni*	before/ahead (of), p. 64, 75
昨日	*sakujitsu*	yesterday, p. 73
昨年	*sakunen*	last year, p. 17
錯乱	*sakuran*	derangement/aberration, p. 48
寒い	*samui*	cold (*adj.*), p. 42
誘う	*sasou*	invite, p. 100
さっそく	*sassoku*	immediately/right away, p. 139
生業	*seigyō*	livelihood/living, p. 53
製品	*seihin*	product(s), p. 18
生活	*seikatsu*	life/living, p. 40
生命	*seimei*	life, p. 53
せめて	*semete*	at least, p. 151
線	*sen*	line, p. 35
背中	*senaka*	(a person's) back, p. 25

鮮度	*sendo*	freshness, p. 53
銭湯	*sentō*	public bath, p. 25
セールスマン	*sērusuman*	salesman, p. 55
写真	*shashin*	photo, p. 19
7月	*shichigatsu*	July, p. 82
仕事	*shigoto*	work/occupation, p. 58
シール	*shiiru*	sticker, p. 35
椎茸	*shiitake*	shiitake mushroom, p. 147
鹿	*shika*	deer, p. 66
しかし	*shikashi*	but/however, p. 98, 143
試験	*shiken*	exam(s), p. 20
式	*shiki*	ceremony, p. 151
信じる	*shinjiru*	believe, p. 115
新婚旅行	*shinkon ryokō*	honeymoon, p. 151
真空	*shinkū*	vacuum (*n.*), p. 139
新鮮	*shinsen*	fresh, p. 30
死ぬ	*shinu*	die, p. 69
知り合い	*shiriai*	acquaintance, p. 99
下着	*shitagi*	underwear, p. 147
失礼	*shitsurei*	impolite(ness), p. 56, 72-77, 92, 146
静か	*shizuka*	quiet/still, p. 28
紹介する	*shōkai suru*	introduce, p. 121
食品	*shokuhin*	foods/groceries, p. 98
食事	*shokuji*	meal/food, p. 79, 87, 100
勝利	*shōri*	victory/success, p. 44
宿命	*shukumei*	fate, p. 95
出張	*shutchō*	business trip, p. 143
そだてる	*sodateru*	bring up/raise, p. 19
掃除機	*sōjiki*	vacuum cleaner, p. 62
そまつ	*somatsu*	coarse/crude/inferior, p. 129
そろえる	*soroeru*	collect (a complete set), p. 52
素晴しい	*subarashii*	splendid/wonderful, p. 138
すきな	*suki-na*	liked/favorite, p. 35
少し	*sukoshi*	a little, p. 75, 115
済む	*sumu*	end/be concluded, p. 20
住む	*sumu*	live/dwell/reside, p. 20
澄む	*sumu*	become clear/translucent, p. 20
素敵な	*suteki-na*	wonderful/nice, p. 85

T

食べる	*taberu*	eat, p. 14, 80
食べさせる	*tabesaseru*	feed (*v.*), p. 81
大安	*taian*	auspicious day (on the Buddhist calendar), p. 151
たいせつに	*taisetsu-ni*	carefully, p. 19
高い	*takai*	high/tall, p. 71
誕生日	*tanjōbi*	birthday, p. 45, 65
頼む	*tanomu*	request/ask, p. 99
確かめる	*tashikameru*	confirm/check, p. 64
手	*te*	hand(s)/arm(s), p. 72
テニス	*tenisu*	tennis, p. 50
天気	*tenki*	weather, p. 78
てんてん	*tenten*	dot(s), p. 35
手伝う	*tetsudau*	help/assist, p. 121
飛ぶ	*tobu*	fly/soar, p. 107
届ける	*todokeru*	deliver, p. 62

トイレ	*toire*	toilet, p. 72
所	*tokoro*	place(s), p. 71
特別な	*tokubetsu-na*	special, p. 151
得意	*tokui*	specialty/forte, p. 71
特に	*tokuni*	especially/particularly, p. 153
泊る	*tomaru*	spend the night, p. 80
友達	*tomodachi*	friend, p. 27, 122
トナリ	*tonari*	next to/adjacent, p. 134
次	*tsugi*	next/subsequent, p. 25
疲れる	*tsukareru*	become tired, p. 58, 75, 126-127
作る	*tsukuru*	make, p. 81
つなぐ	*tsunagu*	connect, p. 35
釣り	*tsuri*	fishing/angling, p. 67

U

ウインク	*uinku*	wink (*n.*), p. 106
伺う	*ukagau*	call on (someone), p. 92
馬	*uma*	horse, p. 66
海	*umi*	ocean, p. 48, 141
運転手	*untenshu*	driver, p. 107
うるさい	*urusai*	noisy/bothersome, p. 28, 76
歌う	*utau*	sing, p. 134

W

若い	*wakai*	young, p. 58
惑星	*wakusei*	planet, p. 31

Y

焼きイモ	*yaki-imo*	roast sweet potato, p. 29
山	*yama*	mountain(s), p. 141
やめる	*yameru*	quit, p. 91
八百屋	*yaoya*	greengrocer, p. 102, 147
呼ぶ	*yobu*	call/summon, p. 138
ヨーグルト	*yōguruto*	yogurt, p. 110
要求	*yōkyū*	demand/requirement, p. 44
お嫁	*o-yome*	bride, p. 112
読む	*yomu*	read, p. 66
よろしい	*yoroshii*	good/nice, p. 14
ゆっくりする	*yukkuri suru*	take it easy, p. 63
夢	*yume*	dream, p. 85
ゆずる	*yuzuru*	turn over(to)/transfer/give way/concede, p. 24

Z

ぜひ	*zehi*	by all means/definitely, p. 18
ズバッと	*zuba-tto*	decisively, p. 135
頭痛	*zutsū*	headache, p. 92

Notes

Notes

Notes

Notes